THE SAGA OF ... ...

THE TALE OF TRISTRAM AND ISOND

The Saga of Tristram and Ísönd

Translated with an introduction

by Paul Schach

A BISON BOOK

UNIVERSITY OF NEBRASKA PRESS
LINCOLN AND LONDON

CONTENTS

A section of illustrations follows page 72.

PREFACE

Because of its unique position in the development of the Tristram story and in the history of Scandinavian literature, the *Saga of Tristram and Ísönd* (*Tristrams saga ok Ísöndar*) is of importance to students of several disciplines. And because of the nature of the story itself, the tragic tale of two hapless lovers whose irresistible longing for each other was fated to find fulfillment only in death, *Tristrams saga* is appealing to a wide circle of readers. It is hoped that this translation of the saga will meet the needs of students and the expectations of laymen.

Begun over fifteen years ago, this translation was completed during recent sojourns in Iceland made possible by grants from the American Philosophical Society and the Research Council of the University of Nebraska, and a Woods Humanities Fellowship. Permission for the reproduction of illustrations from Roger Sherman Loomis's *Arthurian Legends in Medieval Art* (London: Oxford University Press for the Modern Language Association of America, 1938) was kindly granted by Mrs. Roger Sherman Loomis.

PAUL SCHACH

INTRODUCTION

1.

The *Saga of Tristram and Ísönd* occupies a position of singular importance in the development of the Tristan legend, in French–Scandinavian literary relations in the Middle Ages, and in the history of Old Norse literature. It is the only complete member of the Thomas branch of the Tristan story, and as such the Norwegian prose adaptation of the *Tristran* of Thomas of Brittany is essential for the reconstruction of its source, of which less than 3,200 lines are extant. *Tristrams saga ok Ísöndar* is important also for a critical evaluation of the magnificent but unfinished Middle High German epic *Tristan und Ísolt* of Gottfried von Strassburg (ca. 1210)—the truly classical form of the Tristan story and, like the saga, an adaptation of the romance of Thomas.[1] *Tristrams saga* is believed to be the first Norwegian translation of a French romance to be made at the court of King Hákon Hákonarson (reigned 1217–63) of Norway.[2] If this is so, it does not seem unreasonable to suggest that it was the popularity of this work that precipitated the veritable flood of French romances, lays, and *chansons de geste* that poured into the North during the thirteenth century. A measure of the popularity of the *Saga of Tristram and Ísönd* in Scandinavia is the widespread occurrence in Scandinavian literature of names, motifs, and situations connected with the Tristan story. In Iceland, especially, the influence of *Tristrams saga* was persistent and pervasive, for here the story,

1. Two attempts to re-create the Thomas romance are *The Romance of Tristram & Ysolt by Thomas of Britain*, trans. from the Old French and Old Norse by Roger Sherman Loomis, new rev. ed. (New York: Columbia University Press, 1951); and J. Bédier, *Roman de Tristan* (Paris: Société des Anciens Textes Français, 1902). The best English translation of the Thomas fragments as well as of Gottfried's *Tristan* is found in Gottfried von Strassburg, *Tristan*, trans. entire for the first time with the surviving fragments of the *Tristran* of Thomas newly trans. with an Introduction by A. T. Hatto (Baltimore: Penguin Books, 1960). The most detailed comparison to date of Gottfried's version and the saga is that by Eugen Kölbing in the preface to his edition, *Tristrams saga ok Ísöndar* (Heilbronn: Verlag der Gebr. Henninger, 1878).

2. On literary activity at the court of King Hákon, see Henry Goddard Leach's *Angevin Britain and Scandinavia* (Cambridge: Harvard University Press, 1921), pp. 149–264.

in whole or in part, was imitated, adapted, recast, and parodied over a
period of several centuries.[3]

2.

Although the main root of the Tristan legend is embedded in Celtic
tradition (with sizable subsidiary roots extending into Arabic, Germanic,
Greek, and Oriental lore and literature), the literary history of the Tristan
poem is generally thought to begin in France around the middle of the
twelfth century. The earliest stages of this history are obscure, and consequently the question of the nature and number of lost hypothetical
antecedents and of their relationship to each other and to their supposed
derivatives, the existing epics, has been the subject of lively scholarly
debate. Some scholars posit an *Urtristan or *Poème primitif (ca. 1150),
from which the extant poems are believed to derive, either directly or
through an intermediate stage, the *Estoire of a poet named Li Kièvres.
Other scholars question the existence of one or the other or even of both of
these postulated poems. However that may be, during the second half of
the twelfth century, several branches of the Tristan story developed in
France, two of which are of interest to us here—the Thomas branch, mentioned above, and the Béroul branch.[4]

Although Béroul (or a continuator) did not finish his poem until three or
four decades after Thomas had composed his Tristran (ca. 1160), the
Béroul version of the story can be regarded as the "older" one because it is
less sophisticated than the romance of Thomas. In this more primitive
form the Tristan poem was introduced into Germany around 1175 by
Eilhart von Oberge, a vassal of Henry the Lion, Duke of Saxony. Henry's

3. On this see Margaret Schlauch, Romance in Iceland (Princeton and New York:
Princeton University Press and American Scandinavian Foundation, 1934), passim;
Paul Schach, "Tristan in Iceland," Prairie Schooner 36 (1962): 151–64; idem,
"Tristan and Isolde in Scandinavian Ballad and Folktale," Scandinavian Studies
36 (1964): 281–97; idem, "Some Observations on the Influence of Tristrams saga
ok Ísöndar on Old Icelandic Literature," in Old Norse Literature and Mythology:
A Symposium, ed. Edgar C. Polomé (Austin: University of Texas Press, 1969);
and Marina Mundt, "Omkring dragekampen i Ragnars saga loðbrókar," Arv 27
(1971): 121–40.

4. For a recent review of research on the sources of the Tristan legend, see Helene
Newstead, "The Origin and Growth of the Tristan Legend," in Arthurian Literature
in the Middle Ages, ed. Roger Sherman Loomis (Oxford: Clarendon Press, 1959),
pp. 122–33. The most detailed work is Gertrude Schoepperle Loomis, Tristan and
Isolt: A Study of the Sources of the Romance, 2d ed. (New York: B. Franklin, 1960).

wife, Mathilda, was a daughter of Eleanor of Aquitaine, under whose patronage, it is widely held, Thomas composed his *Tristran*. Eilhart is believed to have used the same source as Béroul, and his translation, *Tristrant und Isalde*, evidently remained popular for over a century. The popularity of Eilhart's translation is attested by the fact that Gottfried's two successors, Ulrich von Türheim (ca. 1250) and Heinrich von Freiberg (ca. 1300), based their continuations of his unfinished epic on Eilhart's version rather than on Gottfried's source. The German chapbook *Tristrant und Isalde* (ca. 1350) was also derived from Eilhart, and this *Volksbuch* in turn was the source of five poems (*Meistergesänge*) by Hans Sachs and of his *Tragedia mit 23 personen von der strengen Lieb Herr Tristrant mit der schönen Königin Isalden* (1553). The Czech Tristan poem (ca. 1350) was also derived mainly from Eilhart's translation, although recent studies indicate that this work owes more to Gottfried's epic than was formerly supposed. The tremendous popularity of Eilhart's translation and its derivatives is due no doubt to the dramatic action and the elemental, sometimes even savage passion that characterize and inform this branch of the story.

In marked contrast to Béroul and Eilhart, Thomas recast and refined the story. He expanded the brief account of the hero's parents into a well-rounded prologue that effectively foreshadows the story as a whole. He eliminated much of the crudeness of his source, such as the barbaric episode in which King Mark has the queen cast to the lepers for their amusement. On the other hand, he introduced episodes, evidently of his own creation, such as Tristan's rescue of the abducted queen (chapters 49 and 50 in the saga) and the hall of statues episode (chapters 78–81 and 85). The first of these additions to the story was clearly intended to gain sympathy for Tristan and thus to mitigate his double offense of adultery and infidelity to his kinsman and liege lord. The purpose of the second innovation was to contribute to the modernization and refinement of the elemental passion of Thomas's source into a more delicate, more sophisticated emotion in accordance with the doctrine of courtly love. For Thomas did transform the Tristan poem into a courtly epic to the extent that it was possible with such a deeply tragic story of overwhelming passion. His greatest strength was his delicate and discerning psychological analysis of his characters. He was less interested in their actions than in the motives of their actions. But too much psychology can stifle poetry, and his long passages of dissected passion tend at times to become tedious. Thomas's greatest weakness was his penchant for using reason as a motive for action, for this overrationalization sometimes vitiated passages of inherent poetic beauty or of potential dramatic power. It is difficult, for example, to take Thomas seriously when he asserts that the king banished Tristram from the court because his nephew's behavior toward him was *unreasonable*, or when he has the heroine die because it was not *reasonable* for her to survive her dead sweetheart.

If Thomas can be said to have refined and rationalized the ofttimes uncouth and fiercely passionate Tristan story, Gottfried von Strassburg must be credited with having spiritualized it and, through his formal artistry, with having marvelously transmuted it into a magnificent poem of surpassing beauty. When we read Bédier's complaint that the translator, a certain Friar Róbert suppressed nothing in his translation except the poetry of his source, it is difficult to escape the suspicion that the great French scholar unwittingly attributed the poetic beauty of Gottfried to his source. It is true, of course, that Friar Róbert occasionally pruned so severely as to cut away not only the dead debris of excessive introspection and moralizing but also some of the matter that is vital to the meaning (if not to the plot) of the story. The love-potion episode, for example, whose lyric-dramatic possibilities were fully realized by Gottfried, was treated in a very perfunctory manner by Friar Róbert (chapter 46). On the other hand, the translator seems to have made a few improvements upon his source. In the first of the two innovations mentioned above, for instance, King Mark's primary motive for surrendering the queen to the Irish knight is fear (if, that is, we can assume that Gottfried made no changes in this passage, for the original is lost). In the Norwegian adaptation, however, this motive is toned down, and the king is made to give up the queen in order to keep a promise made in the hearing of the entire court. Similarly, in the hall of statues episode Thomas has the hero alternately flatter and upbraid the likeness of his sweetheart. Friar Róbert, however, has Tristram vent his hatred on the image of the evil dwarf. The purpose of these two changes was clearly the enoblement and refinement of those two characters.[5] Despite these and other deviations from its source, *Tristrams saga* remains, to quote Bédier, "notre témoin le plus sûr de Thomas," and this, as already suggested, is one of several reasons why serious Tristan students need to know the Old Norse version of the story.

---

5. For a discussion of these changes, see Paul Schach, "The Style and Structure of *Tristrams saga*," in *Scandinavian Studies: Essays Presented to Dr. Henry Goddard Leach on the Occasion of His Eighty-fifth Birthday*, ed. Carl F. Bayerschmidt and Erik J. Friis (Seattle: University of Washington Press for the American-Scandinavian Foundation, 1965), pp. 63–86.

3.

According to the Prologue, *Tristrams saga* was written by Friar Róbert in 1226 at the request of King Hákon Hákonarson. The question immediately arises how the Norwegian monarch became acquainted with the *Tristran* of Thomas and why he commissioned its translation at precisely this time. As we have already seen, the Tristan story had been closely associated with the royal house of Anjou since the time of Henry II and Eleanor of Aquitaine. A "sword of Tristran" was numbered among the regalia during the reign of King John, and his successor, Henry III, is believed to have commissioned the laying of the tile pavement at Chertsey Abbey depicting many scenes from the Tristan story. Since King Hákon not only regarded the Angevin court as a model for his own court but also enjoyed a cordial personal relationship with Henry III, it is not surprising that a manuscript of Thomas's *Tristran* should sooner or later find its way to Norway.

This country had enjoyed good clerical, diplomatic, and commercial communication with England for several decades, and during the summer of 1225, the year before Friar Róbert completed his *Saga of Tristram and Ísönd*, trade between the cities of Bergen and Lynn was brisk. Among the trading vessels that sailed between these ports was one belonging to Duke Skúli, the uncle, counselor, father-in-law, and eventual adversary of King Hákon.[6] It was in the summer of this year that the Norwegian monarch sent Henry III a brace of falcons and the promise of more upon receipt of a shipment from Iceland, and the Angevin monarch in return sent King Hákon a gift of grain. It is tempting to connect the *Tristran* manuscript with this exchange of gifts between the two monarchs, and to associate the translation of this epic with King Hákon's marriage to Lady Margaret, Duke Skúli's daughter.[7]

About Friar Róbert not much is known. Some scholars maintain that he must have been an Anglo-Norman because of his name and his knowledge of French literature. Others insist that the style of *Tristrams saga* renders it unlikely that the translator could have been other than a Norwegian or an Icelander. Whatever his nationality may have been, there is general agreement that Friar Róbert is identical with the Abbot Róbert who sometime later translated the *Elie de Saint-Gilles* for King Hákon. Róbert's name has been associated by various scholars with the

6. It will be recalled that the conflict between the Norwegian monarch and Duke Skúli was dramatized by Henrik Ibsen in *The Pretenders*.

7. This question is thoroughly discussed by Leach in *Angevin Britain and Scandinavia*, pp. 36 ff. and 180 ff.

translation of four additional French works, including the *Lais breton* of Marie de France. Until recently this has been largely a matter of speculation or at best of a casual, impressionistic comparison of the style of these four works with *Tristrams saga* and *Elis saga*. A recent study by Peter Hallberg, however, lends substance to this scholarly speculation and establishes Róbert as one of the key figures in the transmission of French poetry to the North during the Middle Ages.[8]

4.

With the exception of the *Strengleikar* (the Breton lays), the six Old Norse translations of French works made by Róbert have been preserved almost exclusively in Icelandic manuscripts. All the manuscripts of *Tristrams saga*, for example, were made and preserved in Iceland. Although the oldest of these date from the second half of the fifteenth century, the *Saga of Tristram and Ísönd* must have been well known much earlier— certainly before the end of the thirteenth century, for borrowings from the saga begin to make their appearance in literary works written around the turn of the century. The nature and number of these borrowings as well as the dates of the manuscripts and of the main derivatives of *Tristrams saga* suggest that this story enjoyed its greatest popularity in Iceland during the fourteenth and fifteenth centuries and that there was a renascence of interest in the saga toward the end of the seventeenth century. Thus there is an interesting parallel between the popularity of the Thomas branch of the Tristan story in Iceland and the popularity of Eilhart's Tristan poem on the continent.

Probably the earliest and certainly one of the most skillful adaptations of a Tristan loan in Icelandic literature is found in the so-called Spes episode of *Grettis saga* (ca. 1300). Based on the theme that great accomplishments do not assure good fortune, this profoundly moving story of the tragic life and death of the Icelandic outlaw Grettir the Strong concludes with the avenging of the hero by his elder brother Thorstein in Constantinople. The account of his vengeance and its consequences is based upon a skillful blending of Tristan themes with loans from an Icelandic biography of Harald the Tyrant (d. 1066), who had served in the imperial bodyguard in Constantinople before winning the throne of Norway. This combination of the equivocal oath motif and reminiscences of King Harald's

8. "Norröna riddarasagor. Några språkdrag," *Arkiv för Nordisk Filologi* 86 (1961): 114–38.

treacherous misdeeds provides an ironic counterpoint to the central theme of the *Saga of Grettir*.⁹

A more obvious borrowing from *Tristrams saga* is found in the *Saga of Rémund the Emperor's Son*, an Icelandic chivalric saga composed about 1340 by a writer who was well versed in saga literature, and especially in the translated romances. Rémund, the son of Richard, emperor of Saxland, falls in love with a woman who appears to him in a dream. When his parents forbid him to go in search of his dream girl, Rémund summons an artist and bids him create a likeness of his sweetheart.

> Shortly after this something strange happened. Rémundr disappeared daily from his men, and this continued for half a month.
>
> And one morning after this, as the king was going to church very early with his bodyguard, he saw a maiden standing in the vestibule of the church, who was so fair and beautiful, polite and elegant, that all believed they had never seen her equal. He went to her and greeted her courteously. But even though the emperor was very powerful, the maiden would not return his greetings, but remained silent.
>
> Then Junkeri Rémundr approached and said to his father: "My dear father, this is not, as it seems to you, a woman created by God, but a statue made in the image of the woman who appeared to me as I slept. And this statue is but smoke and ashes compared with what she really looks like. Perhaps you will be more inclined to have compassion on me, now that you have seen this statue, even though it is worthless compared with her."
>
> The emperor now grew silent and went away without speaking a word. But Junkeri Rémundr took the statue in his arms and kissed it with great joy. And here you can see what ardent love really is. And now a long time passed during which Rémundr found his greatest pleasure in taking the statue with him wherever he went and thus alleviated his distress.

The hall of statues episode in *Tristrams saga*, on which this passage was obviously modeled, had a peculiar fascination for authors of heroic and romantic sagas. The compiler of the *Saga of Dietrich of Bern*, for example, made use of it three times: in the version of the story of Wayland the Smith known as *Velents þáttr*; in *Herburts þáttr*, which has affinities with the Middle High German epic *Biterolf*; and in *Írons þáttr*, where it is combined with a motif from *Aucassin et Nicolette*.¹⁰ In both *Rémundar saga* and *Þiðreks saga af Bern* we find, in addition to adaptations of the hall of statues episode, a whole complex of Tristan traits and situations. The former includes the duel, the sword fragment, the poisoned wound, the

9. For a discussion of the Spes episodē, see Schach, "Tristan in Iceland," pp. 156–60, and "Some Observations on the Influence of *Tristrams saga*," pp. 111–21.

10. On this motif, see A. H. Krappe, "Sur une forme norroise d'un épisode d'*Aucassin et Nicolette*," *Romania* 55 (1929): 260–63.

quest for healing, etc.; in the latter there are four characters named Ísodd. One of them has a son named Tristram, another has a daughter named Ísodd, and the fourth is given to Þiðrek (Dietrich) as his wife after he has slain a terrible dragon. The strong influence of *Tristrams saga* on *Þiðreks saga* is not surprising when we consider that the latter work was compiled in Bergen not long after Friar Róbert had completed his first translation there.

Nor is it surprising that the tragic death of Tristram and Ísönd should have inspired the composition of ballads in Scandinavia. So many details of the death scene in *Tristrams saga* have been preserved in the Norwegian ballad "Bendik og Årolilja" that the only question regarding its relationship to the saga is whether the influence was direct or indirect.[11] Nor can there be any doubt about the ultimate source of the several Danish ballads about Tristram and Ísönd or of the remarkable Faroese "Tistrums táttur" despite the considerable degree of erosion and distortion in these poems resulting from generations of oral transmission. The substitution in the Faroese ballad and in one of the Danish poems of incest for the adultery motif can perhaps be explained on the basis of a scribal error in one of the manuscripts of *Tristrams saga*, where Tristram's foster mother is described as the sister rather than the wife of his foster father.

By far the most artistic poem derived from *Tristrams saga* is the poignantly beautiful "Tristrans kvæði," with its mournfully appropriate refrain *Þeim var ekki skapað nema að skilja*, which means, in a literal translation, "for them it was fated only to sever." Practically unknown outside Iceland, this austerely beautiful "Ballad of Tristran" is the pregnant and artistically perfect embodiment of the tragic fate of the ill-starred young lovers who, despite their irresistible longing for each other, were destined by fate to be completely united only in death.[12]

The derivatives from *Tristrams saga* which reveal the greatest degree of distortion and contamination are the Icelandic folk tales. Nevertheless, they contain enough Tristan survivals and reminiscences to justify their derivation, at least indirectly, from the saga. There is evidence that several of these folk tales may have as their source not the Norwegian translation itself but a condensed Icelandic adaptation of it known as the *Saga af Tristram ok Ýsodd*.

11. This ballad is discussed by Frederick Paasche, *Noregs og Islands Litteratur inntil Utgangen av Middelalderen*, Norsk Litteratur Historie, vol. 1, new ed. by Anne Holtsmark (Oslo: H. Aschehoug og Co., 1957), pp. 517–19.

12. A translation of this ballad is found in *The Northmen Talk: A Choice of Tales from Iceland*, trans. with an introduction by Jacquelin Simpson (London: Phoenix House; Madison: University of Wisconsin Press, 1965), pp. 257–60.

This "rustic" *Tristrams saga*, as Henry Goddard Leach characterized it, was formerly dismissed as an insignificant, clumsy retelling of the story based upon an imperfect recollection of Friar Róbert's translation. A close examination of the text, however, reveals affinities with other romantic sagas besides the *Saga of Trsitram and Ísönd*. This indicates that the author was well read, and that, in turn, suggests that his deviations from the Norwegian translation are not the accidental result of faulty memory but the consequence of deliberate calculation. Although some portions of this Icelandic adaptation appear to be parody, the conclusion of the story indicates that the author's primary concern was the justification of the love of Tristram and Ýsodd. He assures his readers that the trees which grew up from the graves of the hapless lovers "are still standing there as a token that Tristram did not beguile Ýsodd the Fair because of malice against his kinsman, King Mórodd, but rather because God Himself in His wisdom had destined them for each other." Thus the Icelandic tale can be read as a protest against the blind lasciviousness of King Markis and the deceit and duplicity of Tristram and Ísönd in the Norwegian translation. If this interpretation is correct, the Icelandic *Saga af Tristram ok Ýsodd* is in reality an anti-Tristan much like the *Saga of Harald, the Slayer of Hring*, which Margaret Schlauch has plausibly shown "to have been constructed as a deliberate reply to the French romance."[13]

5.

Despite the striking difference between the ornate rhetoric of *Tristrams saga* and the limpid, seemingly simple language of the Icelandic sagas about native heroes, the tremendous popularity of Róbert's translation is not hard to understand. The Sagas of Icelanders were the creation of the twelfth and thirteenth centuries, and the fall of the Icelandic Commonwealth in 1262 heralded the end of this genre as relevant serious fiction. Furthermore, the central problem and spirit of *Tristrams saga* are not foreign to the prose and poetry of the North. Several Icelandic sagas and Eddic lays revolve about the love triangle, and the concept of tragic fate, symbolized by the love potion in the Tristan story, is basic to many sagas and heroic lays. It is this spiritual affinity between *Tristrams saga* and the indigenous literature of the North that accounts in a large part for its enormous popularity during the Middle Ages.

13. Schlauch, *Romance in Iceland*, pp. 150–53. On the "rustic" Tristram tale, see Paul Schach, "The *Saga af Tristram ok Ýsodd*: Summary or Satire?" *Modern Language Quarterly* 21 (1960): 336–52.

6.

A word remains to be said about the manuscripts, editions, and translations of *Tristrams saga*. Despite the popularity of this work, its manuscript transmission is far from good. Extant are two vellum fragments from the second half of the fifteenth century, two complete or nearly complete paper manuscripts from the second half of the seventeenth century, and a somewhat condensed transcript from one of the paper manuscripts from the beginning of the eighteenth century.[14]

To date three editions of *Tristrams saga* have been published. The first of these was prepared by the Icelandic scholar Gísli Brynjúlfsson and appeared in Copenhagen in 1878. The second edition, which was made by the German medievalist Eugen Kölbing, was published in the same year in Heilbronn. Brynjúlfsson based his edition on the paper manuscript AM 543 4to, to which he appended a diplomatic text of leaves one and three of the vellum AM 567 4to, XXII. Kölbing used the same manuscripts, but substituted the material from the two vellum leaves in his text for the corresponding passages in the paper manuscript. A popular edition of *Tristrams saga* in modern Icelandic orthography was published in Reykjavík in 1954. The editor, Bjarni Vilhjálmsson, based his text on that of Brynjúlfsson, but occasionally substituted readings from the paper manuscript ÍB 51 fol. and its somewhat condensed transcript JS 8 fol. A critical edition of the saga based on all extant manuscripts is in progress.

The only complete translation of *Tristrams saga* is the German one by Kölbing appended to his edition of the work. On the whole, it is readable and correct, although Kölbing made no attempt to imitate the ornate, alliterative style of the original. The chief weakness of the translation, aside from an occasional misunderstanding of the original, stems from the fact that the Icelandic text is based on only one manuscript and two leaves of a second one. A comparison of several chapters from Kölbing's translation with the corresponding passages in the present translation based on other manuscripts is revealing. Gísli Brynjúlfsson appended a fairly detailed Danish summary of the saga to his edition. Both J. Bédier and Roger Sherman Loomis based their reconstructions of the *Tristran* of Thomas

---

14. For a discussion of these manuscripts, see Paul Schach, "Some Observations on *Tristrams Saga*," *The Saga-Book of the Viking Society* 15 (1957–59): 102–29; idem, "An Unpublished Leaf of *Tristrams Saga*: AM Quarto, XXII, 2," *Research Studies* 32 (1964): 50–62; idem, "The Reeves Fragment of Tristrams saga ok Isöndar," in *Einarsbók: Afmæliskveðja til Einars Ól. Sveinssonar, 12. desember 1969*, ed. Bjarmi Guðnason, Halldór Halldórsson, and Jónas Kristjánsson (Reykjavík: n.p., 1969), pp. 296–308; and idem, "An Anglo-Saxon Custom in *Tristrams saga*?" *Scandinavian Studies* 42 (1970): 430–37.

primarily on the translation of Róbert, but even so there are significant discrepancies between the two works. Loomis has probably come closer to re-creating the substance of Thomas's romance than Bédier, but his tedious, tortured, archaic language badly distorts and falsifies the style of Róbert.

In the present translation I have tried to remain as faithful to the text as I could without putting too great a strain upon the conventions of the English language. I have retained the alliteration and other rhetorical devices employed by Róbert whenever feasible, and restored alliterative, antithetical, and other collocations wherever it seemed justified. I worked as much as possible from the three published editions, but had before me at all times photostatic copies of all extant manuscripts, including the recently discovered Reeves Fragment and leaf two of AM 567 4to, XII. Like many medieval texts, *Tristrams saga* contains a number of obscure passages. For the most part I tried to render them in a meaningful manner, but occasionally I took the more prudent (or cowardly) course of translating literally and leaving the joy of interpretation to the reader.

In regard to paragraphing, I have tended to follow Bjarni Vilhjálmsson's practice rather than that of Brynjúlfsson or Kölbing. My chapter headings, too, owe much to those in his edition. A close comparison of my translation with the original text will be facilitated by the publication of the critical edition already referred to. The major deviations from the published texts are explained in the papers listed in footnote 14.

THE SAGA OF TRISTRAM AND ÍSÖND

Here is recorded the story of Tristram and Queen Ísönd, which tells of the overwhelming love they suffered for each other. From the birth of Christ 1226 years had passed when this story was written in Norwegian at the behest and request of noble King Hákon. Friar Róbert made the translation to the best of his ability and wrote it down in the words which follow in the story now to be told.

CHAPTER 1

Kanelangres.

In Brittany there lived a youth who was most handsome of body, unexcelled among mighty counselors, and powerful and wealthy in strongholds and castles. He was learned in many kinds of lore, undaunted in deeds of knighthood, trustworthy and high-minded, wise and prudent in his plans, foresighted and foreseeing, fully accomplished in all skills beyond all other men who lived in that country at that time, and the name of this knight was Kanelangres. But to the fierce he was fierce, and to the merciless he showed no mercy. He kept a great host of trusty knights and hardy retainers, and he would gladly have had even more men about him if he had had the means to maintain them. Since he was so gracious with gifts, so considerate in his conduct, and so brave in battle, he soon won such extensive lands and such rich booty from his enemies through his prowess and valor in fighting that within a few years his fame and fortune increased mightily. During the third year in which he bore the arms and armor of knighthood he assembled a huge host and fiercely assailed many a king and duke, inflicting on them severe losses of men and money. He burned down the royal castles and strongholds in that land, and many of the king's knights were overcome and captured, and from all of them he exacted high ransom—gold and silver and jewels, as well as horses and suits of armor. Sometimes he too lost some of his men, as can often befall in battle. Such fierce onslaughts did Kanelangres make against the king, devastating his kingdom and capturing his men, that the king finally sought a truce and parleyed with him in the presence of the most prudent men, and they appointed a time and place for peace transactions between them.

When the terms of peace were agreed upon, Kanelangres appointed a regent over his lands, his castles, and his towns and cities, and over his noble chieftains and faithful knights. Thereupon he made ready to go abroad with a group of followers to make the acquaintance of doughty men and to gain fame and enhance his knightly prowess. Much had he heard told about England—that it was a plentiful and powerful kingdom, beautiful and bountiful, fair and famous, resplendent with noble knights, mighty castles, and powerful strongholds, that its hunting grounds teemed with

3

game, both birds and beasts, and that it was blessed with rich ores of gold and silver, with raiment and apparel and splendid steeds, and with gray furs, ermine, bearskins, and sable. And therefore he thought he would like to see for himself the gentleness and valor, the grace and bravery of the courteous people of that country who bestow honor and accord fine fellowship to all good men who choose to visit them and dwell among them. So, too, he also wished to observe their manner of life, their habits and customs, and to test and try their might and their weapons and their prowess in knightly games.

CHAPTER 2

Kanelangres sails to England.

When Kanelangres had considered these matters, he made ready to journey thence in seemly and fitting fashion, with abundant provisions and handsome companions, but with not more than twenty men, knights who were tried and true as well as prudent and courteous. They were magnificently equipped with excellent weapons, strong armor, and splendid steeds, and thus they came to England, landing in Cornwall.

At the time when Kanelangres came to England, noble King Markis was the sole lord and ruler over all the English and the men of Cornwall. With a large and carefully selected entourage of distinguished men, King Markis had his residence in the capital city, which was called Tintajol. In this city was the most formidable stronghold in the entire kingdom.

As soon as Kanelangres learned that the king was in Tintajol, he set course for that city with his knights. And when he and his companions arrived at the royal palace, they dismounted and entered the hall of the king. Carefully observing courtly custom and conduct, they went two by two, holding each other by the hand, dressed and attired in gorgeous apparel.

When Kanelangres and his companions came before the king, they greeted him with proper respect. And when he had heard and understood their greeting, he replied with dignity, as behooves and beseems a gracious monarch. Then King Markis bade them be seated, placing Kanelangres closest to him and his companions and comrades farther away, in accordance with courtly etiquette. Thereupon the king asked Kanelangres to tell him about himself. And this youth, conducting himself properly and prudently, assured the king that his purpose there was peaceful, and thanked him for his hospitality. With friendly words he told the king whence he had come to his kingdom and why he had wished to visit him. He said he wished to remain in the royal retinue, both to enjoy the hospitable entertainment there as well as to acquaint himself with courtly bearing and courteous conduct. When the renowned King Markis realized that Kanelangres's purpose in coming to his court was to remain there and serve him, he received him and all his companions with fitting distinction, holding them in higher esteem than his own knights; and thereby Kanelangres gained the greatest good luck and surpassing good fortune.

CHAPTER 3

King Markis honors Kanelangres with a festival.

When Kanelangres had been with the king for some time, enjoying such high esteem and honor, magnanimous King Markis, so we are told, had preparations made for a great and glorious feast to celebrate a certain high festival. Now the king sent letters bearing his royal seal to all quarters of his realm, inviting all distinguished men—earls, dukes, and barons—to the festivities, together with their wives, sons, and daughters. And when they had heard the king's request and learned his behest, they all hastened to heed his will and to render homage to him by making ready without delay—counts[1] and earls and other noblemen in the kingdom, as well as

---

1. All extant MSS have *Bretar*, "Bretons," but this is evidently the result of an early scribal error for *Greifar*, "counts."

the rulers of all nearby islands, together with their wives, sons, and daughters in due order.

In accordance with the custom of the country, all these people whom the king had invited now came to the royal festival, and this large crowd assembled in Cornwall in a forest by a certain lake. Here there were lovely meadows, broad and level, bedecked with beautiful blooming shrubs and grasses. And because this greensward was so pleasant and delightful, King Markis had the large tents placed and pitched there—gold and green, blue and red, and richly embroidered with gilt and gold—under fragrant foliage and freshly blooming blossoms. Here newly dubbed knights and other youths engaged in jousts and bohorts[2] and other knightly games without falsehood or folly, and thereby won the admiration and affection of modest maidens and lovely ladies, assembled there in such large numbers both inside and outside the panoplies with their husbands and sweethearts, all of whom had come to attend the festivities.

CHAPTER 4

Kanelangres proves his skill at arms.

Now a host of the most handsome people whom human eyes might wish to see were assembled there. As King Markis sat watching his splendid knights, he was overwhelmed with happiness at the thought that he should be the sovereign ruler over this land, which was so wealthy and powerful and peopled with such chivalrous men and gentle ladies. And because of all these things he pondered now with care and good will how he might arrange and stage this festival so that it would be unsurpassed in magnificence and splendor. Thereupon he had the feast begun, honoring and treating all his subjects and his distinguished guests with the choicest and finest of foods.

2. The bohort was an equestrian exercise in which two phalanxes of knights rode against each other in an effort to penetrate the opposing ranks. The joust was a contest between two mounted knights armed with shields and blunt lances.

When the king had finished eating and all his guests had been seemingly served, the youngest among them proceeded to the aforementioned fields to amuse themselves, and they called to their squires to accompany them with their chargers, for they wished to put their strength and youth to the test. Thereupon the squires appeared with their steeds and armor. The newly dubbed knights and other young men now armed themselves and raced their horses at full gallop and in hard tilts to win the affection of the many maidens, and they marked their weapons so that they might see who was victorious in their mock combats.

But Kanelangres was the most powerful of all in the passage of arms and the most valiant in the jousts, for he knew best how to bear his armor and was most valorous in all feats of knighthood. Here, too, as always, he gained the greatest fame, for all the maidens and ladies in that great crowd cast affectionate eyes on him. All of them desired his love, even though they had never seen him before and did not even know from what country or family he came or what his name was. Yet they inclined their hearts and minds toward him, for that is the way of women. They prefer the fulfillment of their desires rather than moderation, and often desire what they cannot obtain while they reject and neglect that which is theirs to have and to hold. Thus it was with Dido, who was so ardently in love that she burned herself to death when her dearest, who had come from a distant land, deserted her.

Thus misfortune has befallen many who willingly abandoned themselves to such great sorrow.

CHAPTER 5

King Markis's sister.

This renowned and mighty King Markis had a sister who was so beautiful and becoming, lovely and lovable, gracious and graceful, magnificent and majestic that there has not been a flower like her in the world within the ken of man. This precious jewel was well aware, as were all others in the kingdom, that there had never been born her equal in wit and wisdom, courteous conduct, liberal and noble character, so that rich and poor, young and old, miserable and wretched loved this lovely maiden with heart and mind. And as far as men heard about her in other kingdoms, her fame and glory increased, and she gained the affection of many noble rulers and handsome youths who had never even seen her.

CHAPTER 6

The princess suffers grief and distress.

Even though this gentle and modest maiden was endowed with the most gracious decorum and every kind of good fortune, it may well have been true of her, as so often is said, that there is seldom anything without a flaw. Few can know or guess whence that distress came which was now to appear; for shortly after she had seen that man she was assailed by such manifold thoughts, cares, and concerns and a strange affliction that she was unable to remember, recall, or discern what wrong she might have wrought against God or man that such an oppressive fate should befall her, since she had never through word or deed brought harm to anyone, but had always gladdened everyone with her diverting discourse, generous good will, and courteous conduct. It was a great pity that this gentle and genteel maiden was so tortured by such unrest and anxiety as now beset her that, richly attired, as befitted her, she left her tent with a bevy of lovely ladies to watch and view the brisk skirmishing of the knights and other young men.

After she had observed their tilting and jousting for a while, she suddenly caught sight of that most excellent knight Kanelangres, distinguished from all the others in prowess, valor, and chivalry. And when she saw him, and the huge crowd of men and women praised his accomplishments and chivalry, and after she had long regarded his skillful horsemanship and knightly bearing, she was overcome by such pensiveness that at once all her love and desire were completely bent on him. Presently she sighed from the bottom of her heart. She was rent inwardly and her feelings were inflamed, and almost immediately this burning passion leaped into her face. All her natural beauty vanished, and she suffered wretchedness and oppression, but she did not know why. Then she sighed a second time and felt even more burdened, for her heart and limbs trembled so that her entire body broke out in a sweat. She was almost deprived of her wits by this fierce heat which engulfed her, and thus she said:

"Oh, Lord God, where does this strange affliction come from? This cruel distress has a strange hold upon me. I have no pain in my limbs, yet this heat burns me, and I do not know where it comes from. I am afflicted with a severe sickness of such an unbearable nature that I seem to be well and yet I suffer unendurable seizures. Where does this evil come from that injures me so balefully? Is there no physician so skillful that he might give me a healing potion? It scarcely seems possible that it is this warm day that so poisons me inwardly. I would never have thought that this illness could inflict such pernicious distress upon me, so that I shiver from heat and sweat from cold, and yet neither heat nor cold is in itself an illness, but torment and torture for those who have too much of both of them. These two things, heat and cold, combine to torture me, and since neither will part from the other, nor grant me relief, I must needs endure both."

Thus gentle Blensinbil for a long while let herself be torn by sundry torments.

CHAPTER 7

Blensinbil considers her condition.

Presently she glanced at the field below and saw the knights riding swiftly and gracefully across the plain and shattering the strongest spear shafts against shields in spirited tilts.

Now as she watched the knights jousting, her burning passion abated, for the view of this beautiful place and the pleasing sight of chivalrous knights skirmishing assuaged her fiery love and imparted coolness to her excessive ardor. And as she watched the tournament, she left off thinking somewhat and nearly forgot her former mood, for it is the way of love that, even though one's senses are overwhelmed by love's vehemence, this love is much easier to endure if one is occupied with some kind of work or diversion. Thus it was with this young maiden. As she watched the knights tilting, her distress was alleviated.

This was of short duration, however, for as soon as she noticed that Kanelangres proved himself to be more valiant and handsome than the others, the distress which she had previously suffered in heart and mind returned anew with manifold anxiety and abundant unrest.

"Surely," she said, "this man is endowed with sorcery and evil powers, since I am tormented so grievously by the mere glimpse and sight of him. Oh, God, be Thou the shield and protection of my dreadful love, for terrible troubles will come from this knight. And if all who look at him experience the same feelings as I do, then he surely possesses evil arts and venomous torments with which to destroy people—for I tremble all over my body and burn inwardly from the sight of him. There is no denying that he came here in order that I should be tormented on account of him. Oh, Lord God, how can this torment and trouble, grief and distress be taken from me? For it would be more seemly of him to request than for me to offer such things to him, and thus bring shame and disgrace upon myself and my whole family, for he would immediately discover my folly and lack of foresight, and would think at once that I was accustomed to such fickle love affairs and would swiftly and shamefully reject me. But of what use is it to me to lament over such matters, for I am by no means able to do otherwise than to reveal this to him, and then it will prove true of me as of so many others that 'a choice once made is binding.'"

CHAPTER 8

Blensinbil and Kanelangres meet.

When the knights had jousted as long as it pleased them, they left the field. Courtly Kanelangres came riding up to the place where lovely Blensinbil was standing with her becoming bevy of maidens. And when he caught sight of her, he greeted her with fair words.

"God bless you, noble lady!" he said.

She replied at once with a friendly smile, "If you, good knight, will atone for the transgressions you have committed against us, then may God bless and honor you."

When Kanelangres heard the maiden's words, it seemed as though he grew concerned about them, and he thereupon addressed her with these words:

"Gracious lady," he said, "what are these transgressions which you assert that I have committed against you?"

Blensinbil replied, "I think that you are the only one among our men who is aware of your transgressions, and for that reason I am somewhat sad and angry."

Yet she called him back again, for she felt that her heart was powerfully moved by her love for him.

Kanelangres could not understand what she said, for he did not know what matters she had been pondering, and he replied to her with seemly words:

"Lovely maiden," he said, "if it is God's will, I shall make suitable and honorable amends in accordance with your own judgment."

Blensinbil replied, "Under no circumstances will I acquit you of my charges until I know how you intend to make atonement."

After they had finished discussing this matter, Kanelangres received permission to depart and he wished her a good day. The maiden, however, sighed from the bottom of her heart and said to him, "May God in heaven protect and preserve you."

Now Kanelangres rode away, filled with fresh concern about what the transgressions might be which Blensinbil, the king's sister, said he had committed against her and which she wanted him to atone for. He marked and mused over her sigh, but the more he meditated, the less he was able to apprehend what the maiden had said. He weltered the entire day in deep concern; and likewise during the night, as he lay in his bed, he pondered this so much that he found neither sleep nor repose.

CHAPTER 9

Both endure the same grief.

Now both of them bore the same grief and endured the same care and concern, abundant affliction and sufficient sorrow because of their great perplexity. She loved him with the greatest good will, and he loved her with the greatest steadfastness, and yet neither of them knew this of the other.

But since he was wise and well-bred, he considered the time and the hour, how or when he might take up his conversation with her, so that he might best change her attitude. In this, as in all other matters, he proceeded properly and purposefully, for an extremely great difficulty lurked on the other side: if King Markis were to become aware that this young knight, who had recently come to the royal court, entertained such desires and intentions regarding such a noble and closely related kinswoman of his, and that he did so in such a secret manner, then Kanelangres would in no wise realize his desires.

CHAPTER 10

Kanelangres remains at the court of King Markis.

Why need we say more about this matter, since all those who have some understanding must surely know that it is the custom of lovers for both to seek to further their amorous desires as quickly as possible even though it be through clandestine meetings. Thus this courtly couple, with the greatest concord, completely carried out their will, and each enjoyed the pleasant fellowship of the other without slander or reproach, for no one could or might harbor any suspicion about their companionship. They loved each other so ardently and with such artfulness and secrecy that the king never became cognizant or conscious of it, nor did anyone else at the royal court, nor did anyone discern or discover for what reasons Kanelangres desired to remain so long at King Markis's court.

But the king wondered greatly that it should please Kanelangres to remain at his court so long, since he had no possessions there, but rather possessed extensive estates and had highborn kinsmen in another country. But the king was told time and again that Kanelangres had developed a deep affection for his sister, and that he would sue for her hand and accomplish this honorably and with the will and consent of the king. And since Kanelangres excelled all others in all accomplishments which distinguish a noble man, the king would have joined them in matrimony with honorable favor at a great festival if Kanelangres had wished to pursue this matter with the king. And for these reasons it seemed as though he gave them leave to converse together whenever they wished or wanted to.

CHAPTER 11

Kanelangres is wounded.

After a period of time had elapsed, the king with a splendid body of followers set out for a tournament against some other knights. And when they had arrived at the appointed place, they arranged the tournament and carried out the games with great zeal and hard-fought skirmishes. Now a furious bohort was fought with great vehemence, so that no one held back from exerting himself to the utmost. Because of these splendid onslaughts men were killed on both sides, since the most famous and excellent knights had assembled here.

Stout-hearted, valorous Kanelangres charged like a lion savagely into the midst of the host, wounding and killing gallant knights all around him and inflicting great losses on his opponents. And when his only thoughts were of charging forward, he received a great and dangerous wound, for he was pierced almost through and through by a sword, and he thereupon fell half-dead from his horse. This tournament ended with many a chivalrous knight killed or wounded, and a host of them taken captive.

Thereupon Kanelangres's companions lifted the half-dead man up and bore him home. There sorrow and lamentation arose in the entire army. All who knew his fame, high-mindedness, and fine disposition lamented his misfortune.

Now when the king's sister learned of the disaster that had befallen her friend, her distress grew all the more grievous, as it was concealed within her breast; for she could reveal it all the less because of the dread and terror that otherwise awaited her in the person of her brother, King Markis, as well as a host of other powerful men. The more secret her distress was, the more grievous it was.

CHAPTER 12

Tristram is conceived.

This gracious lady and her valiant friend Kanelangres were in a state of great concern and perplexity. And she now considered to herself that if he died in such a manner that she could not see him, she would never find comfort for her distress. She went to her nurse and disclosed and recounted to her her grief and pain and asked her to accompany her. She went there directly and contrived with calm cleverness to do so in such a way that no one knew of it except the one person she wished to, her nurse,[1] who willingly assisted her as she desired.

When she arrived at the place where he was, she made use of the time when the house had been cleaned and cleared and all the people had gone out. And when she saw her loved one wounded, her senses failed her and she sank down in a swoon onto the bed beside him. And now once more were renewed her grief, sorrow, and affliction, her weeping and sadness. After a while, when she had regained her senses, she embraced him and kissed him many times, wetting his face with her tears and saying: "My sweet beloved!" And he forthwith, in the grief and pain of his afflictions, embraced her in ardent love, so that the beautiful lady conceived a child in the anguish of her love.

In such great torments of distress, she because of sorrow and he because of his wounds, they conceived that child who later lived to be a source of grief to all his friends and the origin of this story.

1. All the MSS have *fósturmóðir*, "foster mother"; in the corresponding passage of his *Tristan und Ísold* (lines 1200 ff. in the edition by Friedrich Ranke) Gottfried von Strassburg has *meisterinne*, which means, among other things, "fosterer," "teacher," "nurse."

CHAPTER 13

Kanelangres hears of hostilities.

When they had finished their love-play and their conversation, she returned to her room. He had an excellent physician treat his wounds as formerly. And when he had recovered, a messenger from his country came and told him tidings from his friends and followers that Bretons were harrying in his land, killing his people and burning his towns. When he heard this, he thought it unseemly to delay there any longer, and made the greatest possible haste to have his horses, ship, arms, and equipment for travel made ready. When his sweetheart learned of this, her grief and unhappiness increased.

When he came to her to take leave for his voyage home, she said to him, "I am indeed your sweetheart, and I have loved you unwisely, for I shall surely die for your sake unless God grants me mercy, for after your departure I shall never attain happiness or the hope of comfort. Sadly I lament my love for you, and now I am faced with more abiding sorrows. I do not know which of these two sorrows I shall choose, for I am filled with grief at your departure, and I am fearful that you might remain here even though you then could often comfort me. But if I were not with child, it would be easier for me to remain here and my grief would be gentler to bear. If you go away, then I shall regret that I ever saw you. Yet I would prefer to die, rather than that harm should befall both of us, for you do not deserve such a death. But I deserve to die for your sake rather than that you, my dearest, should be slain innocently. Therefore your departure is a great comfort to me, since you will not suffer death from remaining here. For then our child would be fatherless, whereas it will receive honor and distinction from you. It grieves me to see your dexterity and chivalry and knightly accomplishments. I have deceived myself, and therefore I am lost and undone." Thereupon she swooned and sank into his arms.

Somewhat later, when she regained consciousness, weeping and lamenting, he comforted her. He had her sit down beside him and dried her eyes and face and said, "Dearest, I will do whatever I can in this matter and whatever is most beseeming for both of us. I did not know anything about the circumstance which you have just mentioned. Now that I know about it, I shall do what is most honorable. I shall either remain here with you, although that is dangerous, or else you will accompany me to my native land, where I shall treat you with all the honor befitting our love. Now choose and consider, my dearest, whichever is pleasing to you."

CHAPTER 14

Kanelangres and Blensinbil sail to Brittany.

When Blensinbil perceived Kanelangres's kindness, and his desire to take her with him to his native land, or, if she would rather remain, his willingness to abide by that wish also, she knew that he deserved no reproach since he wished to do her will in so honorable a manner. She said to him tenderly, "My delight and my dearest, we cannot remain here in freedom. You must know for certain that if we stay here, we will live in grief and peril."

For this reason they decided that she should accompany him to his native land.

Thereupon Kanelangres took leave of the king for the voyage home and hastened to the ships, where he found his men gathered together and in readiness.

Then they raised the mast, hoisted the sail, and got a good wind. They arrived safe and sound in good time and landed in Brittany.

When Kanelangres came into his realm, he found his people in dire straits because of his enemies. He summoned his countrymen and his steward, whom he knew to be faithful and devoted to him, and told them about everything, including his sweetheart. He entered into legal and consecrated matrimony with her and celebrated it with a great and glorious festival. Then he sent Blensinbil secretly to a strong and powerful castle. There he had her guarded for a time in honorable and seemly fashion.

CHAPTER 15

The birth of Tristram.

One day Kanelangres armed himself and rode into battle to recapture the towns and strongholds of his realm with great zeal. There was no lack of heavy blows. Many a shield was battered and broken. Some men were smitten, some wounded, and some killed on both sides. Vassals and knights were captured and taken prisoner.

In this great battle courtly Kanelangres was pierced through and hurled from his horse dead to the ground. All his men were saddened, and they bore his body back to the castle. Then there arose there weeping and wailing with divers cries of lamentation and they found no other comfort than to bury him with honor.

But his beautiful wife was afflicted with such grief that no one might comfort her. Often she fell down in a swoon, lay as though dead, and because of her raging grief tried to kill herself, refusing all consolation. Dead was her joy and all her pleasure. She would rather die than live, saying, "I am more wretched than all other women. How shall I live after the death of such a magnificent hero? I was his life and solace, and he was my dearest and my life. I was his delight, and he was my joy. How shall I live now that he is dead? How shall I be comforted, when my joy is buried? It is fitting that both of us should die. Since he cannot come to me, I must pass through death, for his death beats upon my heart. How shall I be able to live here longer? My life must follow his life. If I were free of this child, I would follow him in death."

As she thus vented her grief, refusing all consolation, she fell unconscious onto her bed, and the birth pangs began to torture her. Now she suffered both grief and torment, and she endured these pains until the third day. And during the night following the third day she gave birth to a beautiful boy with great pain and weariness, and died, after the child was born, because of the great grief and torment she had endured and the fervent love she bore her husband.

Now the grief of the court attendants increased. Friends bewailed their lord, others their lady. All mourned for both of them. Now grief awakened in the halls among the courtiers because of the death of their magnificent lord. Still greater was the sorrow in the sleeping chambers among the maidens for their dead lady. All wept who saw the boy so young fatherless and motherless.

CHAPTER 16

Tristram is christened.

Now when the marshal learned of the fate of his beautiful lady, he said that the child should be christened so that it might not die unchristened. Then the priest brought the chrism and administered it to the child and asked what its name should be. He said, "It seems advisable to me that in view of the grief and affliction, the care and torments, the anxiety and unrest, the sore and many sorrows, and the distressing event which has befallen us through his birth that the boy be named Tristram." For in this tongue *trist* means *sorrow* and *hum* means *man*. And the reason his name was changed is that *Tristram* sounds nicer than *Tristhum*.

"The reason he shall be named thus," said the marshal, "is that he was born to us in grief. He has lost joy and gladness—his father, our lord, and his mother, our lady—and therefore it beseems us to grieve that he was born in sorrow and distress."

He was then christened and given the name Tristram, and he received this name because he was conceived in sorrow, carried in distress, and born in the afflictions of grief. All his life was filled with sadness. He well deserved his name, for he was sad when awake, sad when he slept, and sad when he died, as those will learn who continue to listen to this story.

Then the marshal secretly had the child taken away from the castle to his own home, where he had it protected in a worthy manner and yet in secret from its enemies. He did not want to reveal to anyone that the boy was the son of his lord. He bade his wife[1] go to bed, and after some time had passed, he had her go to church and announce that she had conceived

---

1. AM has *systur*, "sister," but the writer of ÍB, after copying *systur*, superimposed *konu*, "woman," "wife," over it.

the child and had given birth to it at that time. For he did not want the king to learn that this was the son of his lord. If the king had discovered this, he would swiftly have had the child slain so that the king should not suffer hostilities or harm, the loss of his men or danger to his kingdom. And for that reason the steward had the boy reared in secret and had him protected in gentle care and honored as his own son.

CHAPTER 17

Tristram acquires skills and accomplishments.

Here you may hear of noble deportment and manly and courteous conduct, for the true and trustworthy marshal was wise and benevolent— he made his lord his son in order to protect him from trouble, to shield him against his enemies, and to honor him with dignity. Later he had him taught the knowledge of books, and Tristram was most eager to learn. He was instructed in the seven arts, and he became fluent in all kinds of languages. Then he learned to play seven kinds of stringed instruments so well that there was no one who was more distinguished and skilled in this than he. No one was more highly endowed than he in kindness of heart, generosity, and courtly conduct, in intelligence, wise counsel, and valor. In good manners and distinguished deportment he did not have his equal, and his excellence continued to increase. When his foster father recognized his excellent qualities, he honored him with the choicest garments, splendid horses, and all kinds of entertainments, and with whatever kindness he could grant him with due deference and devotion, so that his sons grew angry and wondered why their father loved him so dearly and esteemed him more highly than he did them with fondness and all kinds of honor, services, and favors, and with especially affectionate tenderness. The reason they became angry with their father was that they thought that Tristram was their brother.

CHAPTER 18

Tristram is abducted by Norwegian merchants.

It happened one day that a large seagoing vessel put in and anchored in the harbor below the castle. On board were Norwegian merchants with a large cargo, and they had been driven there by long-lasting gales from the north. The cargo included much fur-stuff, ermine pelts and beaver pelts, black sable, walrus tusks and bearskin cloaks, goshawks, gray falcons and many white falcons, wax and cowhides, goatskins, dried fish and tar, train oil and sulphur, and all kinds of Norwegian wares.[1] And when news of this came to the castle, the marshal's sons discussed it, and called Tristram to them.

They said to him, "What shall we do, seeing that we have no falcons for our sport? But now many very beautiful ones have come on this ship. If you want to be of help to us, you can attain whatever you wish to ask of our father, for he and mother never deny you anything you ask for. They would rather buy you seven of the finest than to see you distressed." And they begged him urgently until he consented to help them.

Then they all went to the ship and had the birds shown to Tristram. But the merchants were Norwegians and understood neither Breton nor French nor any other language in which to conclude the transaction. Tristram, however, was conversant with several tongues and he bargained with them for seven birds. His father paid for them and he gave them to his brothers.

Then he noticed a chessboard there and asked if any of the merchants wished to play chess with him; one of them agreed to do so, and they set and agreed on a high wager. When his foster father saw that Tristram was sitting at the chessboard, he said to him, "My son, I am going home, but your tutor will wait with you and accompany you home when you are ready." And a courteous and well-mannered knight remained there with him.

But the merchants were astonished at the young man and praised his understanding, his skill, handsomeness, and ability, his intelligence and

---

1. The list of "Norwegian wares" seems to have been expanded somewhat by Icelandic scribes. Sulphur was an important Icelandic export item in the Middle Ages, as were also falcons, dried fish, and train oil.

the manner in which he defeated them all. They considered that, if they were able to abduct him, they would stand to gain greatly from his abilities and great knowledge; and also, if they wished to sell him, that they would receive much money for him.

As he sat there, intent on the game, they secretly loosened the lines and weighed anchor and let the ship drift out of the bay. The ship was covered with an awning, and since it drifted before the wind with the tide, Tristram did not become aware of it until they were far from shore. Then he said to the merchants, "Sirs, why are you doing this?" They replied, "Because we want you to come with us."

At once he began to weep and wail loudly. He bemoaned himself, and the knight bemoaned him also because of his affection for him. And then the Norwegians seized his tutor, put him into a boat, and gave him one oar.

Now the sail was hoisted and the ship was under way at full speed, and Tristram, filled with grief and anxiety, was in their power. With much exertion and great difficulty his tutor made land, nor was he particular in his choice of harbor or landing place. But Tristram remained there in grief and anxiety, and he prayed that God in His mercy might keep and protect him from peril and distress, so that he might not perish from weapons or winds, from deceit or disgrace, or from the falsehood or faithlessness of heathens, nor be delivered into their dominion. He sighed deeply with fear and sorrow and pitiful lamentations.

Now his tutor arrived at the castle and announced tidings which brought joy to no one. This great host—one thousand persons—was afflicted with grief and concern at the news of Tristram's abduction. When this news became known, the entire court grew sorrowful, and the whole household hastened down to the sea. The grief of Tristram's father was as great as that of all the others combined, so that he could scarcely contain himself. He wept and lamented this great loss, declaring it was all his misfortune that this disaster should befall him and this great sorrow beset him through such an unfortunate circumstance.

And he gazed out on the sea and cried in a loud voice: "Tristram, my comforter and my lord, solace of my heart and mind, my love and my delight, to God I commend you, and into His care and keeping I commit you. Now that I have lost you, life holds no consolation for me since we are apart."

So pitifully and often and continuously did he vent his grief and bewail his Tristram that all who were there, young and old, wept and prayed for him. All who were fond of Tristram and had taken delight in him, both rich and poor, were now saddened and sorrowful. All who knew him throughout the entire realm were filled with grief. Sad were all the people who were in his realm, and sad the new passenger on the ship, who was known and beloved to all.

CHAPTER 19

Tristram and the merchants in peril on the high seas.

But the marshal of the castle grieved for him most of all, and he had a ship made ready to put to sea without delay with full rigging and ample provisions, for he wished to pursue the merchants and never to return alive unless he had ascertained for certain where his foster son Tristram had been taken. Now he hastened as much as he could, and soon the ship was fully rigged and provisioned with wine and food. Thereupon he went on board, had the anchors weighed and the ropes drawn in and the sail hoisted, and put out to sea. They set course for Norway, and endured toil and tossing on heavy seas, hunger and discomfort, and fear and affliction in foreign lands. They came to Denmark and Sweden, to Norway and Iceland, to Orkney and the Shetlands to search for their lord Tristram, but they found him nowhere.

For when his abductors were approaching their homeland, a sharp head wind caught their ship with furious gusts and sea currents so that they would have perished if they had not struck their sail at once. The sea was agitated by huge waves, and it hailed and rained with thunder and lightning. The mast was high and the sea was deep, and the ship listed so strongly from the violent gale that no one could keep his footing, and they turned the ship and let it drift with the storm. And now the entire crew became so frightened and distressed that they broke out in tears and pitiful lamentations, and even the hardiest among them were filled with dread, and all feared that they must perish, for they were in the most dire straits. All week long they were swept along by the tempest and the driving wind so that they saw land nowhere, nor did they get a favorable wind. Therefore they were constantly in fear and terror, nor did they know in which direction lands or harbors lay.

Then all the crew addressed the captain. "This storm," they said, "and all this rough voyage and peril which we are enduring have befallen us as our own deserts, for we sinned against Tristram when we tore him away from his kinsmen, his friends, and his country. This storm will never abate, nor will we ever make land as long as we keep him aboard. Now if God will forgive us and have mercy on us and give us a favorable wind so that we might reach land, then we promise that in turn we will set him free." And all of them agreed to this and confirmed it with strong handclasps.

Immediately the darkness disappeared and the sun began to shine and the tempest to abate. And they took heart at once and rejoiced. They hoisted sail, and after they had been sailing for a short while, they caught sight of land, and they sailed toward it with billowing sail and a fair wind. They anchored close to land, put Tristram ashore, gave him a little of their own provisions, and prayed God to give him good fortune. They did not know in what country they had set him ashore. They hoisted sail immediately and went on their way.

CHAPTER 20

Tristram meets two pilgrims.

Now Tristram was in a strange land, frightened and forlorn. He sat down and gazed at the ship sailing away with full sail, nor did he want to leave there as long as he could see the ship. As soon as it had disappeared from sight, he began to look about him, saying with anxious mind:

"Almighty God, Who in Thy might hast created man in Thine own image, Who art one God in three persons and three persons in one Godhead, have mercy on me and give me counsel, and shelter me from evil designs and dangers, from peril and from enemies, for Thou knowest what I am in need of. For I know neither where I am nor to what country I have come. Never before have I been so perplexed and destitute and helpless. While I was on the ship with the merchants, I had the comfort and cheer of their companionship as long as we were together. Now I have come to the shores of a foreign land. From here I can see nothing but forests and mountains and valleys, sheer cliffs and crags. From here I can see neither roads nor paths, nor any human being. I do not know which way to turn, nor what course of action to take, nor do I know whether this land is Christian or pagan, inhabited or uninhabited. Here I am ignorant of everything except my own helplessness. I can find no one to give me help or comfort, or to teach me the manners and customs of this country. I can find here neither paths nor guides. It may be too that I do not know the language of the people, if indeed there are any human beings here. I am afraid that lions might rend me, or bears bite me, or some other living creatures that do not fear the human voice or have never seen a human being.

"Alas, my father has lost me! Alas, my mother is weeping for me, my friends are grieving for me, my kinsmen are wanting me! Curses on the birds that I desired so much to buy, and on the chessboard on which I was victorious! I am sorry for my friends. If they knew that I am alive, then this knowledge would comfort them. But I know it does no good to lament this. What help is it to me just to sit here? It is better for me to go away as long as daylight lasts and I can see how to direct my steps. Perhaps I shall have the good fortune to come upon some habitation where I may find shelter in my need."

Thereupon he climbed up a certain hill, where he found all kinds of man-made trails, and he happily followed one of them out of the forest. He was very tired by then, but he pressed on as fast as he could. He was clad in magnificent garments, and his form and figure were splendid. The heat was oppressive, and so he took off his cloak as he walked and carried it over his shoulder, thinking often of his friends and kinsmen and praying God's mercy for himself. His mind was filled with anxiety.

Presently he espied two pilgrims making their way along the same path. They had been born in Veneasarborg and were returning from the mountain of the great Michael. They had made a pilgrimage to that place to offer up their prayers. When they met the lad, he greeted them courteously and they returned his greeting.

"Friend," they said, "to whom do you belong? What are you doing, and where do you come from?"

Tristram perceived that they were not natives of that country, and he answered them craftily so that they might not learn for certain how he came to be there or why he was on foot there.

"Friends," he replied, "I am from these parts and I am looking for my friends, but I can't find any of them. We were hunting here today, and they pursued the deer, while I remained behind alone. They must soon come along on this road, for it is the one on which we rode away from home. Now tell me in what direction you are going and where you plan to spend the night. Perhaps I should like to join you."

They replied, "We wish to take lodging in the city of Tintajol."

Then Tristram said, "I also have an errand to perform there, for which I have the reliable support of friends, once we get there this evening. If it is God's will, we shall find good lodging and powerful friends, who will show us ample good will."

CHAPTER 21

Tristram instructs the huntsmen.

Now they all proceeded together, Tristram and those who accompanied him. Tristram asked them the news of other countries and events of chieftains, kings, and earls. And as they were telling him this news, a stag bounded past them with a large pack of dogs in pursuit—bloodhounds and greyhounds, some baying and some barking, but all in hot pursuit. The stag saw that it would not avail him to flee further. He turned onto the path in front of the pilgrims, and then he leaped out into the river and followed the current. He tried to regain the path, but when the dogs attacked him, he turned back into the river. And when he came to land again, they overtook him and pulled him down. Presently the huntsmen arrived and found the stag lying there. They raised him up on his legs and prepared to strike off his head.

Thereupon Tristram said, "What are you going to do? I have never seen a stag broken up in such a way as you want to do it. Tell me the method and manner in which you are accustomed to dress your game."

The chief huntsman was courteous and modest and well accomplished in all of the customs of courtly behavior. He saw that Tristram was a very handsome and splendidly attired youth and in every respect of manly appearance and he said to him: "Friend, I shall be happy to tell you our method. When we have flayed our game, we split it along the back and cut it into quarters. We have never learned or seen or heard nor have we acquired from elsewhere any other usage. Now if you know of a better way that we have not yet seen, show it to us and we will gladly adopt it."

Tristram replied, "May God reward you. But that is not the custom in our country, where I was born and reared. Because I sense your good will toward me, I shall show you the usage of huntsmen in my native land if you will make me your foreman."

Then he made ready to break up the stag. When he had stripped the skin off of the animal, he dressed it. He first removed the genitals and cut the hams from the backbone. Next he removed the entrails and detached both shoulders as well as that portion of the back between the shoulders that is fattest and the portion between the loins that is fleshiest. Then he turned the stag over and cut away both flanks and all the fat that was in it and thus severed the forelegs from the back. Then he cut through the neck and severed the head and likewise the tail with all the fat of the loin. Thereupon he cut a large branch and fastened to it the heart and kidneys, the liver and loin and lungs and spoke thus to the huntsmen: "Now the stag is broken up according to the custom of our huntsmen. Prepare the quarry for the hounds." But they did not know what that was. So he took all the entrails he had removed from the stag and laid them on the hide and brought the dogs and gave them these to eat. Then he cut some of the flesh from all four legs and threw these on the hide also, and the dogs ate all of it. "This is called quarry. The hounds are to eat this from the hide." And this seemed strange to the huntsmen.

"Now," he said, "prepare your pole present. Fasten the head of the stag to the pole and present it to the king in courtly·fashion."

The huntsmen replied, "By my faith, people in this country have never before heard mention of quarry or pole present. Since you are the first huntsman to bring us this usage, demonstrate this capital and courteous craft, for we do not know how to follow this practice."

Then Tristram went into the forest and cut down as large a pole as he could carry in one hand and tied to this pole the branch on which he had placed the choicest delicacies that he had taken from the stag and fastened the head of the stag to the top of it and said to the huntsmen: "Sirs, take this. This is called the pole present. Take the head to the king in a courtly manner, and have your lads precede you, and blow your hunting horns.

This is called the gift of the chase. That is the custom of huntsmen in the country where I was born."

They replied, "We do not know how to go about this. Yet we think more highly of your usage than of our own. Accompany us into the presence of the king and bring him the gift of the chase, and we shall do everything you request."

Thereupon they set Tristram on a horse, and with his pilgrims following him, he carried the head of the stag on the pole and soon came to the royal palace.

CHAPTER 22

Tristram displays his accomplishments at court.

Then Tristram took a hunting horn and blew a long and beautiful fanfare, and all the huntsmen blew their horns as he had instructed. There was a large body of them with many horns, and there was a great flourish of horns. And then a great crowd of royal retainers and servants came pouring out of the hall, and asked in astonishment what that loud blowing of horns might signify. But Tristram and the band of huntsmen did not cease winding their horns until they had come before the king himself. And then the huntsmen told the king in what manner Tristram had dressed and broken up the stag, and how he had given the hounds the quarry, and about the pole present and how, sounding their horns, they were supposed to bring the game to their lord and king. For never before in that country had a stag been broken up in such wise, nor had the catch of huntsmen been carried home in such a dignified manner, nor had the king been honored so seemingly by anyone.

As Tristram now remained in the royal retinue, he often went on the chase and always broke up the stags and the other game which he brought down in the same way, and brought them to the king according to his

custom, for no other usage was better or nobler than the one Tristram had
learned in his native land, and the king's huntsmen considered his usage
better than theirs.

Now when the king had finished his evening meal, his retainers took
their places in the hall to amuse themselves—some at the chessboard,
others at draughts. Some listened to singing, others to stories, but the
king listened to the playing of the harp. Tristram recognized the tune and
the melody at once and said to the harpist: "You play that melody well.
That lay was composed by the Bretons in Brittany about the sweetheart
of good Geirnis."

The harpist said, "What do you know about it? Have you ever had a
harp teacher? In what country did you study music, for it seems to me
that you understood this song?"

"Good master," replied Tristram, "I studied the harp somewhat for my
own amusement where I used to live."

"Then take the harp and let us hear how well you have learned."

Tristram took the harp and tuned all its strings. He played such a lovely
lay for the king and his men that the king and all who heard it marveled.
All expressed praise at how well he had learned and what a well-educated
man he was, endowed with manifold mildness and goodness of heart and
many kinds of entertaining talents. He displayed splendid virtuosity.
Never in their lives had they heard the harp played more beautifully.

When he had finished the lovely lay, the king and many others requested that he favor them with another performance on the harp. And
since he found that it pleased them, he played them a second lay of a
different kind. He tuned the harp again and played the second lay, singing
in tune with the harp. In a little while he played a third harp melody with
such grace that they all enjoyed and praised it.

Then the king said to him, "Good friend, praise be to him who instructed
you and so wisely trained you. You shall spend the night in my quarters
and comfort me with your accomplishments and your music as long as I
lie awake."

Thereafter Tristram was welcome among all the people there. He was
agreeable and affectionate, cheerful and kind, and amiable to all. He was
dear to all, but dearest to the king. He had charge of his tracking hounds,
his bow and quiver, and for this the king gave him a horse. He accompanied
the king during the day for his diversion, and at night he served him with
harp-playing. Now he richly enjoyed the benefits of having learned so
much as a child. If Tristram had not been abducted, he would not have
become acquainted with the king nor so well liked and highly esteemed in

the country where he now was—known and dear to all in that city and throughout the entire realm.

CHAPTER 23

Concerning Marshal Róaldur, Tristram's foster father.

Now let us be silent about Tristram and relate something about his foster father, that gallant marshal who traveled far and wide, scouring many countries in search of his foster son, enduring wind and wave, storms at sea and ocean gales and the severe distress of exile, without hearing any tidings of Tristram.

When he arrived in Denmark, three years after his departure from home, he learned from a certain wayfarer that Tristram was at the court of King Markis, a famous and powerful prince, and that he was highly esteemed and honored, dear and beloved by all, and that he should remain with the king since the king was well pleased with him. When this man had told him such tidings, he believed him immediately, for he recognized from his description of Tristram's apparel that he had told the truth. This man was one of the pilgrims who had accompanied Tristram and had gone to the royal court with him. And as further proof, he knew everything about Tristram—his conduct and how he had secured the king's love and affection.

Now Róaldur the marshal wished to continue his journey, and he boarded a ship and waited for a favorable wind. When the wind came up, he set out on his voyage and sailed over the sea and landed in England. Then he proceeded to Cornwall, which borders on the western part of England. Here the king was in residence with his retainers. Róaldur inquired secretly whether anyone could give him reliable information. They told him the welcome news that on that day Tristram by chance was to serve the king at table. Róaldur was extremely eager to have a private meeting with Tristram. Until recently Róaldur had enjoyed wealth and authority, but now he stood there in wretched rags—his destitute appearance was due to his long and arduous journey. He did not know how he might bring it about that Tristram would see him, for he was miserably clad and had little money for suitable attire, so that he might appear perfectly presentable at court. Now he was sad, for a poor man is not welcome at the court of a king, for only those are welcome there who are sufficiently wealthy. Even though a man be of a good family and well mannered, he will find few persons at court who will help him if he is poor.

Now Róaldur had arrived at court, although none welcomed him, for no one knew who he was or on what errand he had come. But finally it occurred to him that it would avail him nothing as a stranger to conceal his identity any longer from such a king as resided here, and so he approached the outer door and called the guard. He gave him a gift to let him enter without restraint. When the guard saw the gift, he opened the door, took him by the hand, and led him to the hall. The guard entered, but Róaldur waited outside.

Tristram came out when the guard called him. As soon as Róaldur caught sight of Tristram and recognized him for certain, he fell down in a swoon, so greatly did he rejoice at his coming. All those who accompanied Tristram wondered why this man, sinking down for joy, should so lament his happiness. They took hold of him and raised him up. But weeping and rejoicing together grieved and comforted Róaldur, giving him such great happiness that never before had he felt such delight as he now came to experience when he saw that Tristram was there. As soon as Tristram recognized him, he welcomed him with kisses and embraces so that no one can describe how each one of them loved the other.

Then Tristram took Róaldur by the hand and brought him to the king, saying openly, in the hearing of the entire court: "Sire, this is my kinsman, father, and fosterer, who has searched for me in many a land. Now, having found me, he is joyful. He has been tossed about on the high seas for a long time, and now has the appearance of a poor man. I shall rejoice at his coming if you will receive him cordially."

The king was gracious and cordial and called a page to him secretly and said to him: "Accompany this man to our sleeping chamber and serve him well and give him a rich set of garments such as you can see will suit him well, for he has always been a wealthy man, prudent, polite, and accomplished. He shall be treated honorably in our land, for he was a great companion and joy to Tristram."

When Róaldur was clad in courtly fashion in splendid attire he looked like a man of rank with well-shapen limbs. Before he had looked like a peasant churl, but now he appeared to be a yeoman or an earl.[1] He was assigned a place at the king's table, and sat there now, a mighty man among mighty men. Now they dined with pleasure, and Tristram waited upon him according to courtly custom.

CHAPTER 24

Tristram and Róaldur return home, and Tristram slays Duke Morgan.

When they had eaten and drunk as much as they pleased of fine food and delicious drink, they told tidings of other countries according to the custom of the court, what events had occurred among princes who ruled in neighboring lands and what had happened in recent years that it was seemly for them to know and for Róaldur to tell.

Thereupon Róaldur, with eloquent speech and well-chosen words and keen memory, reported to the king in the hearing of the entire court in what manner Kanelangres, his lord and ruler, had secretly abducted Blensinbil, the king's sister, whom he loved, and how he had married her, and his death, and how she had borne him a son, and her death, and why he had named the child Tristram,—and he showed him the golden ring with precious stones that King Markis's father had owned and that the king had given his sister because he loved her with seemly affection,—and how Blensinbil had requested before her death that he should give the king, her brother, that finger ring as a true token of her death.

When Róaldur had surrendered the ring and the king had received it, the king recognized the youth by the ring. And then in the entire assembly of dukes and earls, vassals and knights, cup-bearers and shield-bearers, ladies and maids, there was no one who did not shed tears because of this

---

1. Hann sýndist áður sem einn *akurkarl*, en nú er hann sem einn höldur eða *jarl*. This is a typical example of rhyme, as employed by Friar Róbert occasionally in *Tristrams saga* and in his other translations.

distressing event, and also because he told them the distressing story of how Tristram had been stolen from him and how he had searched for him in many countries with trials and tribulations.

When the king had duly heard this news, he called Tristram to him with words of affection and embraced him with a warm kiss as his beloved kinsman and nephew.

Then Tristram approached his kinsman, the king, and fell on his knee before him and said to him: "Sire, I want you to provide me with armor, for I wish to visit my native land and patrimony and to avenge the death of my father. For I am now old enough to be able to seek to regain my rightful property."

Then all the nobles, who sat on both sides of the king, declared that it well beseemed him to do so, and the king consented and commanded that armor be prepared for him. This armor, which the king gave him, was very good, and was largely made of pure silver and gold and set with precious stones.

Brave, handsome, courteous, powerful, and polite knights were assigned to Tristram. They fastened spurs made of pure gold to his feet; this was done by two vassals. King Markis himself girded him with a sword and gave him a mighty blow on the neck and said, "My dear nephew, never take a blow from anyone else unless you avenge it at once. Accept no other reparation or redress except a blow for a blow as long as you can revenge yourself. Thus will you do honor to your knighthood."

The king then made him a stately knight, and a beautiful, powerful charger was led forth for him, caparisoned with red trappings woven with gold and with figures of lions on them. That day the king gave him horses and armor for twenty young men for his benefit as well as one hundred additional proven knights, all of whom were to accompany him to the south of Brittany to demand and defend his rights.

In the morning Tristram took leave of the king for his voyage home with his foster father and his followers. They came to the ships and embarked with their horses and weapons. Some weighed anchor and others hoisted the sails, which were of various colors—yellow and blue, red and green. They put out to sea and made land where they had intended to, in southern Brittany.

When they had entered the harbor, they landed before a town called Ermenía and saw there a large, beautiful castle, so strong that it was unassailable in any manner. This castle had been owned by Tristram's father, and it was still held by his men, his retainers, who were bound to him by oath. Marshal Róaldur was the first to go ashore. He rode to the castle, and had all the castle gates and entrances opened. Thereupon Tristram rode up with his retinue, and Róaldur presented him with all the keys to the castle. Then he wrote to all the vassals of the country that they should come there and welcome their lord, whom he had journeyed so long to find and had found with God's guidance and providence. When the dukes and nobles, the landed men and powerful knights assembled, Tristram received them as his retainers and accepted their oaths of allegiance. And now all the people of his realm rejoiced anew at his homecoming. All the people who had been angry and afflicted when he was abducted were now free and joyful.

On the following morning Tristram set out with twenty knights to go to see Duke Morgan to demand from him the rights and the realm which he had wrested from his father. When he entered the duke's hall, his entire retinue was sitting there. Tristram addressed the duke in this manner in the hearing of all: "God bless you, duke, in like manner as you have done to us, for you wrongly hold my realm after having killed my father in battle. I am the son of Kanelangres, and I have come to demand from you my hereditary land, which my father owned and which you now hold. I demand that you surrender it up to me honorably and freely. In return I am prepared to render you whatever service is proper for a free man."

The duke replied, "I have been reliably informed that you were in King Markis's service and that he gave you good horses, armor, costly stuffs and silks. And I see that you are a handsome knight. But you declare that you want to receive your realm from me, that I wrongly hold your estates, and that I slew your father. Now, I do not know how your request will turn out, except that it seems to me that you are seeking to provoke a quarrel with me, and it may be that you will make such charges as you will not be able to bring to a final issue. If you wish to gain your realm, you will have to take it by force, for I do hold what you call your realm, whether rightly or wrongly. And as for accusing me of the death of your father, in that matter you will have to muster your full strength, for we will never deny nor conceal his death from you."

Then Tristram said, "Whoever kills a man and admits his guilt is obligated to make redress to his friends. You now confess both that you wrongly hold my realm and that you have slain my father. I demand that you redress both, for you can deny neither."

Then the duke said, "Be silent, churl! You are full of arrogance. You are the son of a harlot and don't even know who sired you. You are lying about your father."

Then Tristram grew angry and said, "Duke, now you have lied, for I was born of a lawful marriage. I will prove it to you if you dare pursue the matter further."

When the duke heard Tristram's words calling him a liar, he sprang up, full of anger and malice, and rushed at Tristram and struck him in the teeth with his fist as hard as he could. But Tristram drew his sword and struck him on top of the head, cleaving it down to the eyes, and hurled him dead to the floor in front of him before the eyes of all the Duke's men. Tristram's companions and attendants were most courageous. They swiftly drew their swords and cleared a way through the throng of people in the hall, hewing on both sides and killing anyone they could reach.

As soon as Tristram came out of the hall, he sprang on his horse, and likewise all his companions, each on his horse. They took their shields and spears and rode out of the castle in battle array, and anyone who now dared vex them was a fool. They turned the skirmish into a battle, in which more than a hundred men fell before they parted, for now all the followers of the duke armed themselves to avenge the death of their lord, and five hundred men, all armed, set out in pursuit and galloped so swiftly after Tristram and his company that those with the swiftest horses overtook them.

CHAPTER 25

Tristram entrusts his realm to Róaldur and returns to England.

Tristram had slain Duke Morgan and many of his knights and now was hastily making his way homeward. But a great host of Bretons pursued him and threatened him, declaring that they would avenge their lord. When those who were in the vanguard overtook them, Tristram and his men turned against them and set upon them so valiantly that they killed them all and captured their horses. So completely did they avenge this vexation that the vanquished never gained any glory.

On that same day Marshal Róaldur had sixty knights arm themselves with trusty weapons and good horses and sent them on the same road on which Tristram had ridden forth. They were to lend him support in case he should need it or in case he intended to visit some of his other castles so that he might travel about safely and without fear of his enemies.

Those who pursued Tristram did not know where he would seek shelter, and he swiftly and frequently turned against them and slew those who were nearest. Thus they pursued him for a long time.

Finally the sixty men sent by Róaldur came galloping toward them. They lowered their lances for the attack and immediately afterwards hewed so doughtily and valiantly with their swords that they overran the vanguard and slew all who dared face them. The remainder ran away, and Tristram and his men pursued them and slew them as they fled like a flock of sheep. They took many horses and all kinds of armor as booty and returned to their stronghold with great renown after the victory.

Tristram was a most valiant man. He gained fame and praise, was generous and well liked by everyone, and was a splendid, lordly nobleman of good fortune.

Now he had avenged his father in this victorious battle with great fame, and he then sent for all the nobles in his realm. And when they came there, he addressed them. "Friends," he said, "I am your lawful lord, the nephew of King Markis. And since he has neither son nor daughter as a legal heir, I am his only lawful heir. I now wish to go to him and serve him as fittingly as I can. Now I give to Róaldur, my foster father, this town with all its revenues, and after his death his son shall receive it. This is in return for the toil and trouble which Róaldur endured for my sake as well as for the faithful care and the honorable treatment he accorded me in my childhood. All of you be faithful and obedient to him. Herewith I bestow upon him my right and my rank. Now I wish to depart in friendship and with your leave." And he kissed all of them with tearful eyes.

Then he mounted his horse, and his men likewise, and rode to the ship. They weighed anchor, set sail, and put out to sea. But his subjects remained behind, filled with distress, lamenting his departure, and they were dissatisfied that he did not wish to remain with them and they longed greatly for his return. Now they suffered grief anew because of his second departure from them.

CHAPTER 26

The Irish exact tribute from England.

Now the story of Tristram tells us here that the Irish at that time were exacting tribute from England, and that they had done so for many years. For the Irish greatly loved England because the English king who reigned then was unable to protect himself, and therefore England was tributary to Ireland for a long time. Formerly a tribute of three hundred pounds of pennies was paid to the king of Rome.[1] The first tribute that the Irish took was brass and copper, the second year it was pure silver, and the third year it was refined gold, and this was to be kept for common needs. But in the fourth year the king and nobles of England were to assemble in Ireland to hear the laws, to dispense justice, and to fulfill the punishments of all men.[2] But in the fifth year the tribute should consist of sixty of the most handsome boys who could be found and delivered up, whom the king of Ireland desired as his male servants. Lots were cast among the vassals and other nobles, as to which ones should give up their children. And those on whom the lot fell had to surrender them as soon as the tribute was sent for—even though it might be an only child.

Tristram landed in England in the port which he had chosen in the year in which the king of Ireland demanded the child tribute, and he who had come to claim them had come to land in a magnificent merchant vessel.

In Ireland there was a powerful champion, huge and ill-willed, a strong and fierce man, who used to come to England every summer to claim the tribute. But if the tribute were to be denied him, he would engage in single combat to take it by force from the one who refused it, for one either had to pay the tribute or else face him in battle.

Tristram disembarked, mounted a horse, and rode up to the castle where the king and his dukes, earls, vassals, and a host of knights were already present, for they had been summoned there. The foremost women of the land had also come there with their sons, and it was to be decided by lot which of them should be delivered as tribute to Ireland. All the women

1. The MSS have *Rónia konungi*, "King Rónía," which is clearly a scribal error.
2. This sentence seems hopelessly confused. According to Gottfried, Irish envoys were sent to Rome every five years to receive instructions regarding the dispensation of justice and the conduct of the courts of law. See *Tristan und Ísold*, lines 5979–6002.

lamented because of their grief and distress. Each one feared for her son that his lot would be drawn, for it was of no avail afterward to resist or regret it. And they had good reason to be distressed at such tyranny which forced them to deliver their children into banishment and danger and misery. It is a great misery and a miserable thought that children of such distinguished lineage should be surrendered into thralldom and slavery.

Lord God, Thou art patient to suffer such things. Have compassion for these sad people in their sorrow. Strong men wept. Women wailed and lamented. Children shrieked. The mothers cursed the fathers of their children because they did not dare to protect them from misery against those who wanted to take the children. They called the fathers frightened, disgraced, defeated, and overcome because they did not dare to fight against Mórold, who demanded the tribute. They knew that he was most harsh and fierce, powerful and untiring in wielding weapons, formidable in fighting on horseback, and large of stature, and therefore there were none present who did not choose to surrender their children into thralldom and bondage rather than to invite certain death. The reason that no one dared to fight against Mórold was that no one had any hope of victory.

When Tristram entered the hall, he saw there the great assembly of the most distinguished men in the entire kingdom. All were venting their grief because they had to pay such tribute. Tristram saw their sorrow and sadness, and that many were weeping. He asked what the reason was for their lamentation.

"It is because of the tribute," they replied, "that Mórold, the emissary of the Irish king, is accustomed to take and has now come to demand and exact from the nobles of this kingdom, who are all assembled here to choose by lot which children are to go."

Tristram had been sad when he had entered the hall of the castle, and now he grew even sadder to see the highest nobles of the land down on their knees before those who should draw the lots, each one beseeching God in his mercy to prevent the lot from falling on him. The mothers of the children wept, and the children wailed and cried aloud.

It was at this moment that Tristram, the benevolent, arrived and said in a loud voice: "Noble lords, may God bless you all and free you from your bondage and serfdom, your shame and disgrace. It seems strange to me that, among such a host of knights as I see assembled here, there is no one who dares defend your freedom or to free you from thralldom and bondage by contending in single combat on this day in order to snatch you out of this degradation that oppresses you, so that never again will lots have to be drawn, or your children abandoned to thralldom. In truth, this country is now inhabited by thralls unless you free yourselves from thralldom. For if Mórold carries off the tribute, you are all thralls and not knights, and your country will be pillaged and plundered. Your lack of courage seems to me so great that you are unconcerned where your children will land in wretchedness and dishonor once you have surrendered your power over them. Now, if you will heed my counsel, you will neither send your children away nor pay tribute to the emissary. Choose from your number the one who is the manliest and fiercest in the passage of arms, completely proven in knighthood, and powerful and bold in the wielding of weapons. Let him oppose in single combat the one who demands tribute, and he will surrender, conquered and overcome, on the field of battle. But if no one can be found who is better than I, then for the sake of my kinsman, the king, I shall gladly fight in single combat with such strength as God has granted me. Although Mórold is strong, God is mighty to help me and to free your children and win your freedom rather than that he should depart in such a manner with your children and your property, untried and untested, and carry away your wealth and your heirs. Now stand up at once and cease what you are doing. Never shall Mórold boast that he found us all lacking in courage."

CHAPTER 27

Tristram disputes with Mórold.

Now King Markis spoke. "Many thanks to you, my dear nephew. Come here and embrace me. If you regain our freedom, you shall be the heir to my entire kingdom. No one here is more worthy than you to have it. You are the son of my sister."

Then Tristram went and kissed his kinsman, the king, and all the vassals and knights who were present. And then he handed the king his glove to confirm the duel with Mórold. And all thanked him, young men and old, and said that he would defeat the enemy of his lord and restore their freedom, and then they would all love him and serve him and honor him as their lord since he was willing to be their lord and protector.

Then Mórold was summoned. He believed that they had finished casting lots and that he was to receive the boys.

When Tristram saw Mórold enter and take a seat, he spoke with a loud voice: "Hear, lords and nobles, vassals and knights, young men and old, who have assembled here! Mórold has come here and declares that you have to pay tribute because he is accustomed to collect tribute from you every year. But that tribute was levied against you as unlawful seizure by force and tyranny. The Irish came to England to harry and wage war, and the inhabitants of this country could not defend themselves or secure peace against them in any other way than by submitting to pay tribute, and this has been so ever since. But tyranny is not justice, but lawlessness and an obvious shame and injustice. Therefore it is not right to pay the tribute, since it has always been exacted wrongfully, for it was always surrendered under duress and fear of pillage if this be justly judged. All goods that are seized with robbery everywhere are ill-gotten, and since robbery is wrong, Mórold shall not wrongly have anything from us. Now if Mórold wants to take away the children, that will never happen with our consent."

But Mórold declared he had a right to take them.

Tristram said, "Your very own words show that you have no right to collect tribute and take it away from here, for we shall resist with force and not desist unless compelled to by force. What you want to take by force we will defend with force and not surrender it unless forced to do so. Let him win who has the better cause! We'll teach him to understand that everything they judged to be truth was falsehood."

Now when Tristram had finished saying this, Mórold sprang to his feet and remained standing. He appeared red of face, tall of stature, and stout of limb, and altogether powerful. He spoke in a loud voice from his thick throat.

"I understood," he said, "what your foolishness prompted you to say. You do not want to pay the tribute and surrender it to me graciously, but rather to withhold it from me by force. I am not prepared now for a pitched battle, because I have only a small force of men with me. When I landed in Cornwall, I did not think I needed an army or that you would refuse me the tribute and break your oaths and repudiate my just claims. But since I have so few men and am not prepared for battle, let one of your men meet me in single combat to prove that you are not obligated to pay tribute to me. And if I fail in this, you will rightly and honorably be free.

Now if any one has the courage to take up your cause, let him accept my glove."

Tristram was sitting nearby, courageous and stately, handsome and bold in speech. He arose at once and went to Mórold and said, "This is he who will represent our cause against you, that we are not obligated to pay tribute to you and that we have never broken our oaths to you. I will defend it and prove it against you personally. Quickly get your weapons, for I shall quickly get mine to prove this to be true."

CHAPTER 28

Tristram slays Mórold in single combat.

Now the pledge between the two to engage in single combat was confirmed. Mórold went down to the seashore and armed himself. Then he mounted a large horse that was clad in trusty mail and hung over his shoulder a twenty-pound shield, hard and huge and thick. He girt on a large, keen sword and then rode to the dueling ground, where he galloped his horse, with all the people watching, to demonstrate his riding skill.

Tristram armed himself in the king's castle. He put on good iron cuisse and greaves, and two vassals bound his golden spurs to his feet. Then he put on a trusty coat of mail, thick and large. His kinsman, the king, girt him with a good sword, which had been proven in many battles. He had been given this sword by the king, his father, together with the finger ring that you have already heard mentioned in this story. These were the two most precious possessions in the kingdom. Then they placed on his head a bright, shiny helmet, the best that could be found. They hung on his shoulder a trusty shield, bound with iron and decorated with gold, and led forth a sorrel horse, well covered all over with mail. Tristram mounted the horse and took leave of the king and all his friends. All feared for Tristram. They implored God's mercy for him and commended him to God Almighty that He might deliver him out of this peril and grant them the freedom which the entire country was in need of. All prayed for him. Thereupon he hastened to seek combat with his enemy to protect and defend the freedom of all England against the emissary of the king of Ireland.

Mórold was strong, stout, haughty, and of great stature. He feared no knight in the world. He was the brother of the queen of Ireland, and demanded the tribute on her behalf. The king had sent him to England because he knew that no man had the power to withstand him. And now the time had come for this to be tested.

First he held his shield before him for protection. Then he lowered his bannered lance for the attack, struck his horse with his spurs, and raced at a gallop toward Tristram. Tristram immediately turned his own shield to cover himself and held his lance for the attack. When they met, each struck the shield of the other with such great force and hard charge of horse that both their lance shafts were shattered, but their shields were so sturdy that they did not break. Thereupon they drew their swords and rained heavy blows on each other, so that sparks of fire flew from their helmets, their swords, and their coats of mail. Tristram was bold in battle, but Mórold was burly and huge and seasoned in many fierce fights. Whenever one left his guard open, the other assailed him, trying to inflict harm on him. Their helmets were dented by their swords, their mail coats were slashed, their shields cloven, and the field was bedecked with iron and steel and the golden ornaments of shields and helmets. Neither the Irish nor the townsmen could clearly see which of them fought better or who had greater hope of victory.

Then Tristram grew very angry. He brandished his sword and delivered a blow down upon Mórold's head, right between the shield and the helmet. The blow cut off the shield strap and the helmet rim and a fourth of the shield with its gleaming gold and gems. It sliced the mailcoat off the arm and as much flesh as the sword reached, and cut through the saddle bow and more than a span down into the horse's back. This blow would have inflicted greater harm on him if the sword had been longer. But Mórold struck at Tristram at the place where he was unprotected, for he held his shield too far from him. The sword struck him on the left side of his chest. The mail coat failed him under the blow, and the sword inflicted a severe wound, so that Mórold came very close to killing him.

Then Mórold spoke to him. "Now it is proven," he said, "that you are pursuing a wrong course. It would have been better to have paid the tribute," he said, "than that you should be so badly dishonored and disgraced, for all the wounds my sword inflicts are mortal wounds because both edges have been poisoned. You will never find a physician who can heal that wound except my sister. She alone understands the properties and potency of all herbs and of all kinds of medications which can heal wounds. Surrender and declare yourself vanquished in battle, defeated and overcome. Then I shall accompany you to the queen because of affection for you and have her heal your wounds. Then let us always be companions, and all my wealth shall be at your command, for I have never found any knight whom I can praise so highly as you."

Tristram replied, "Not for any of the services you offer me shall I betray my merit and my manliness. Much rather will I die in single combat than lose my honor in disgrace. Never will I behave so basely because of any wound, as I think I can still prove to you. God is almighty to help me and to defend our freedom against you with his mercy. I am confident that I shall yet revenge myself upon you. I shall repay you blow for blow, so that England will always be free and safe from you. Now you rejoice, but at evening you will not give praise."[1]

All the townspeople, men and women, were downcast and dolorous when they saw Tristram's horse all covered with blood, and they implored God that He should save him from torment and peril. Tristram heard their words, and then he caught sight of Mórold about to attack him, and he swung his sword with great strength and struck him on top of the helmet. The iron gave way, the steel split, and the war hood was of no avail. The sword sheared off his hair and beard, and remained embedded in his skull and brain. Tristram jerked the sword toward him—he wanted to have it in readiness in case he needed it—and he pulled the sword to him with all his strength. Then a piece of the sword—as much of it as had penetrated—remained embedded in the skull. But Mórold plunged dead from his horse.

And then Tristram said to him, "It may be that Queen Ísodd knows how to heal poisoned wounds and that no one else can help me, but she will certainly never be able to help or heal you. Whatever may become of my wound, your wound is uglier and more hideous."

Then he commanded Mórold's companions to convey his body to Ireland and to make known that never again would the Irish collect tribute from England, neither gold nor silver, except for this gift. Then the Irish took his body and bore it with deep sadness down to the shore.

---

1. *Þú ert nu fagnandi, en að kveldi ert þú ekki leyfandi.* Mislead by Kölbing's misinterpretation of this passage, Roger Sherman Loomis translates "Now art thou full of joyance, but this night thou shalt no more be on live." This sentence seems to be based on the ancient proverb *At kveldi skal dag leyfa,* "Give praise to the day at evening," attributed to Óðinn in the *Hávamál* (Words of the High One).

In his tent they removed his armor, and then carried his body out to the ship. They drew in the ropes, weighed anchor, and put out to sea. They sailed home to Ireland, and there told tidings that caused the Irish much grief.

CHAPTER 29

The Irish bring Mórold's body home to Dublin.

Now Tristram rode back to the royal palace. And they removed all his armor and sent for the best physicians to be found in the kingdom, for the wound was poisoned. He drank theriaca and potions prepared from all sorts of herbs, and they had plasters placed on the wound to draw out the venom.

Now Tristram was in great distress, and the king and his court and the people of the land were in great sorrow, for they feared that he would die. His wounds turned black, and neither herbs nor potions brought healing. They prepared a pleasant dwelling for him and hung it with drapes of precious satin so that he might lie there comfortably.

Now the Irish had entered the best harbor, that of Dublin, and they placed Mórold's body on a shield and carried it through the street. And there was much weeping among all the people at the death of Mórold, the brother of their beautiful Queen Ísodd. All the people said, "The tribute was demanded in vain." Then the emissaries took the body and bore it up to the castle, and vassals came running toward them to see the dead knight.

The emissaries spoke to the king with loud voice and bold words. "Markis, the king of England, sends you this message, that he is rightfully obligated to pay you no other tribute than this dead knight. But if you again demand tribute and send an emissary there, he will return him to you dead. A certain young man in that country, the nephew of the king, bold and valorous, surpassed the valor of Mórold and presented him to us dead, to our sorrow. He has recently joined the royal retinue. No one can be found more valorous than he."

As the king gazed at the dead Mórold, he sighed from the bottom of his heart and was deeply distressed, and the entire court gave vent to their sorrow.

Presently beautiful Ísodd heard these tidings. She left her chamber and went into the hall. When she saw her dead kinsman, she fell upon his body in a swoon and greatly lamented his death, cursing England and the English tribute and Mórold's misfortune. Then she cursed the knight who had slain him, and the entire country that was to pay the tribute.

Then they saw that part of the sword that had broken off and had remained imbedded in his skull. They took a pair of tongs and drew out the fragment and gave it to Ísodd. She had the blood and bits of brains washed off and then placed it in a small chest as a reminder to all of their sorrow, for it was with this that he had been slain. Thereupon they shrouded his body in the most seemly manner.

CHAPTER 30

Tristram is healed in Ireland, and Ísönd enters the story.

And now we must tell about Tristram. He had his wound bound and treated, but he could find no one in the country who knew how to heal him. The wound caused him so much distress that he would rather have been dead than to live in such pain. Never could he find rest or sleep, for the poison had penetrated into his flesh and bones. His friends and kinsmen were very loath to be near him because of the stench that came from him.

Then Tristram spoke to the king. "Sire," he said, "I beg you for the sake of your affection for me, comfort me in my wretched condition, and give me counsel in my misery. None of my friends or kinsmen wish to visit me or to see me or to comfort me. Therefore I wish to go away, wherever God in his sublime mercy may let me come to land in accordance with my need."

When Tristram had finished speaking and lamenting his troubles to the king, the king said, "It is a great folly, my dear nephew, for you to want to kill yourself. In one day an event may occur that ordinarily cannot come to pass in twelve months, so that help might come to you in a brief period of time. But since you wish to depart, I shall have a ship made ready for you with everything you will need to take along."

Tristram thanked the king, but the king and all the others were ill pleased at his departure.

Now Tristram's ship was supplied with sufficient provisions and with whatever else he needed. All the people accompanied him down to the ship, lamenting his departure. They sailed away, and out onto the high seas. Those who remained behind all prayed that God should guard him and be merciful to him.

The ship was driven by winds and waves on the high seas so long that they did not know where they were sailing, but they finally came to Ireland. When they were told where they had chanced to arrive, Tristram was fearful that, since he had come to that country, the king and his enemies might discover who he was, and so he gave himself the name Trantris.

Now he began to demonstrate his mastery of the harp, and the courtly and courteous demeanor of which he was capable, and news of his pleasing appearance and accomplishments quickly spread.

When Princess Ísönd, lovely and gentle, heard these tidings about him, she strongly desired to see him and some of his varied accomplishments, and she asked her father and mother to have Tristram summoned. The maiden Ísönd employed great cunning to persuade her father and her mother, Queen Ísodd, that she should become his pupil, for she wanted as soon as possible to learn to play the harp and to write letters and to compose poetry. Tristram came to the queen's apartment, but no one could bear to be inside because of the stench that came from his wound. The queen found this distressing, and she said to him, "I shall gladly help you for the sake of my daughter Ísönd, so that you may teach her as best you can with kindness and consideration anything she wishes to learn of that which you know."

Then she spoke to one of her attendants: "Quickly prepare some remedies against poison."

She had a poultice placed on the wound all that day, and this quickly drew the stench from the wound. On the following night the queen set to work and with her own hands washed the wound with medicinal herbs and then bound it up with a marvelous poultice, so that in a short while she was able to remove the inflammation and the venom. In the whole world there was no physician who possessed such healing lore, for she knew how to heal all kinds of sores or sicknesses that afflict people. She knew the power of all those herbs that have medicinal qualities. She knew all the methods and means of helping that belong to the art of healing. She knew how to help against poisoned drinks and to heal poisoned wounds and dangerous fevers and to draw all sorts of inflammations and pain from all limbs, so that nowhere was there a master who was more skillful and better than she.

When she had opened the wound and cut away all the dead flesh and completely removed the poison, all the living flesh looked better. Then she applied poultices of sinsing and healing ointments so continuously and vigorously that within forty days Tristram was so well healed as though he had never been wounded. He had completely recovered and was as strong as he had been before. Then Tristram endeavored day and night with all his powers to teach Ísönd to play the harp and other stringed instruments, to write and compose letters, and to acquire all kinds of knowledge and accomplishments. Ísönd learned very much from him. Throughout the entire kingdom her praise and renown increased because of the manifold knowledge she had learned from him through attentiveness. Her mother rejoiced that she had acquired such excellent accomplishments and widely famed wisdom. It was a great joy to her father also that she had learned so much in such a short time, and he sent for her to play the harp for his pleasure and that of other nobles. Then she demonstrated her wisdom in many kinds of questions and opinions that she expressed before the wisest men. She was the king's greatest joy night and day, for he had no other children but her, and she was his greatest comfort.

CHAPTER 31

Tristram plans to leave the country.

When Tristram felt that he was healed and in perfect health, and had regained his flesh and full strength and handsome appearance, he thought much about how he might escape from Ireland, for he dared not remain there any longer. He feared that people there would discover who he was and where he was from, or that he might encounter someone who by some chance would recognize him. He devised a carefully considered plan, and on the following day he went to the queen, knelt before her, and spoke to her with elegant and affectionate words:

"My gracious lady, I bring you the thanks of God and all the saints for your condescending endeavors and benevolence, and for your gracious services and majestic gentility, for you have healed my wound, consoled my disconsolate heart, and graciously treated me. I am devoted to you and at your disposal in service, and I am obligated in every way to venerate you in perfect friendship and steadfast affection. Now with your leave I wish to return home to visit my friends and kinsmen. As long as I live I shall be at your service, but my kinsmen and friends do not know where I am or where I have come to or whether I am alive or dead. When I sailed away, I intended to go to Spain where I wished to study astronomy and other matters which are still unknown to me. But now I want to visit my friends and alleviate their grief. Have my ship made ready so that I may depart with your leave. May God thank you and reward all your good deeds that you have generously and mercifully performed on my behalf to the full extent of my need."

Then the queen said, "My friend, your ship will be made ready at once if you wish. This is our reward for nurturing a foreigner. At the time when we most want to keep you, you desert us for the sake of your friends and count for naught our great efforts, which we have put forth on your behalf. Since you no longer wish to serve us, we will not detain you by force. You shall have your ship, fully prepared and provisioned, as soon as you wish to sail, with God's leave and ours, wherever you like. Now at parting I shall give you as subsistence money a mark of pure gold."

Tristram accepted the gold and thanked the queen for her manifold kindness, gentleness, rich gifts, and abundant goodness. But if the queen had been able to prevail, she would have preferred that he remain rather than depart so quickly.

Now Tristram took up his harp and entertained himself with it as he walked toward the ship. The ship was completely supplied with all the things he had need of. Thereupon Tristram boarded the ship, received a favorable breeze and put out to sea.

CHAPTER 32

Tristram arrives in Cornwall.

Tristram had such a fine voyage from Ireland that he landed in Cornwall just where he wanted to, in the harbor beneath the king's castle.[1] Those who were outside the castle immediately recognized Tristram's ship and at once leaped into a boat and asked where Tristram was. They found him well and cheerful and cordially welcomed and greeted him. He went ashore, and they brought him a large, strong horse. He mounted the horse and rode up to the castle. The king's servants came running to welcome him, and young men and old rejoiced with such gladness as though he had returned from the dead.

When the king heard the news, he rose to his feet at once and went to welcome him and greeted him kindly and embraced him. When the king had seated him beside himself, Tristram told him about his travels— where he had been and who had healed him. Tristram told the king that he had found help in Ireland and that he had contrived clever lies and artifices for his benefit, and that the queen herself had healed him in a gracious manner with potent medicines. All in the king's retinue who heard this marveled at these tidings, for all had thought him so infirm

1. The MSS have *Bretland,* "Brittany," but this is clearly a scribal error for *Kornbretland,* "Cornwall." Kölbing and Loomis write "Bretland" and "Britain," respectively. The corresponding passage in Gottfried's *Tristan* (lines 8223–25) reads *er vuor von dannen zEngelant, | von Engelanden al zehant | ze Curnwale wider heim.* ("He sailed from there to England, from England straightway back home to Cornwall.")

and disabled when he went away that he would never again return or see them again. Some said that he must possess marvelous lore or magic crafts to be able to escape such enemies. Others said that he knew how to change men's minds. And some said that he would revenge himself on all those who had abandoned him in his sickness.

Earls and knights, vassals and the most powerful men in Cornwall now came to fear Tristram because of his wisdom and wiles. They feared that he would succeed his uncle as king, and that he would then strongly oppose and wreak vengeance on those who had so shamefully abandoned him in his illness and wretchedness. Then they plotted against Tristram in secret, for they feared him and envied his goodness, intelligence, and kindness. Thereafter they disclosed that they had decided that it behooved the king to marry and produce an heir, either a son or a daughter, according to God's will, who would succeed him and rule the kingdom after his death. They all assembled before the king and disclosed their decision to him. They asserted and affirmed that unless he married in the near future a woman with whom he could have an heir to rule the kingdom after his death, it was to be feared that war would break out and that someone who had no right to rule the realm would usurp the throne. And for that reason, they added, they did not intend to serve the king any longer unless it pleased him to accept their advice.

Then the king said, "I thank you for your good will and for being so concerned about my present and future honor that you want me to take a wife and produce an heir to rule over my kingdom after my death. I know that you need have no fear of hostilities, yet it is good to be certain and secure. Since this redounds to my honor, I shall gladly comply with your counsel. Find me a princess who is my equal in descent, intelligence, and courtly conduct, pleasing appearance and gentility, chastity and dignified demeanor, so that I need not marry beneath my station. Then I shall be happy to do as you request. You are my sworn vassals, and it is not seemly that your counsel should go contrary to my will."

"Then give us time, sire," they said, "to consider, and appoint a definite day for this matter, and we shall make such a desirable choice that we shall not merit discredit from you but gratitude and complete good will. Since you have entrusted this decision to us and our discretion, we shall make such a choice for you as you yourself would wish."

The king replied, "I shall be happy to comply. I shall grant you a respite of forty days. At the end of that time you will disclose your decision to me. And if it pleases me, I shall gladly comply with it if it leads to a good marriage."

CHAPTER 33

The king agrees to ask for the hand of Ísönd.

When the appointed day arrived, they all appeared before the king, for they were intent on Tristram's downfall, since people seldom leave a man in peace whom they earnestly desire to hate. They now wanted the king to take a wife with whom he might beget an heir. But the king under no circumstances was willing to marry anyone unless she was his equal in descent and prudent and polite in manners and knowledge and also distinguished and praiseworthy. The only reason he was wary of their counsels was that he did not want to marry anyone except the kind of woman who has just been described.

"Lord king," said one of them, "this is the day on which you instructed us to name the woman it beseems you with reason and honor to have as your royal spouse, who is not of lower birth than you, and whom you have requested us to choose. You have often heard that the king of the Irish has a beautiful daughter, so endowed with natural good fortune that she lacks neither the kindness nor the magnificence which it beseems gentlewomen to possess. She is the most renowned and beautiful, the most intelligent and refined in every respect of all women of whom people have knowledge in all Christian lands. Her noble descent is not unknown to you—that she is the daughter of royal parents. Now if you do not want to marry this maiden, it will seem to us as though you did not want to take a wife and produce an heir for your kingdom. It is known to your nephew Tristram, and he will bear witness to it, that we have chosen for you the finest bride we know of, for her excellent qualities are so great that they surpass our ability to describe them."

The king remained silent for a time, considering his reply, before he spoke. "If it should be," he said, "that I did want to marry this woman, how could I ever reach her, since her father and all his men hate me and all my people so much that they would like to kill every living person in this country? I fear that if I sent my men there, he would have them dishonored and killed and would deny me his daughter. This would bring scorn and contempt upon me, such a disgraceful rejection as this, and my enemies would say that it was our terror of him that cowed us into suing for his daughter's hand."

"Sire," said one of the vassals, "it can often happen that kings in various kingdoms go to war against each other with enduring grief and multiform sorrow and loss of life. Later their anger and hatred abate, and they transform enmity into peace and dejection into affection because of sisters and daughters and into the worthiest friendship for the sake of the offspring of their two houses. Now if we might bring about this union and marriage with peace and amity, then it may well happen that you will come to rule all Ireland, for Princess Ísönd is the only child of the Irish king."

The king said, "If that were possible, and if it could be furthered and carried out honorably, I shall marry no one else but Ísönd, for Tristram has highly praised her gentility and wisdom and all the qualities that befit a woman. Now give some thought to how we might win her, for I will never take another if I may not have her."

Then one of the earls spoke. "Sire," he said, "no one in the world can obtain her except your kinsman Tristram. He knows the king and the maiden, and he is on friendly terms with the queen. He knows the Irish tongue and is acquainted with all of Ireland. If he will undertake this endeavor, he can surely obtain her with artifice, by secret or forceful abduction, if the king will not willingly give her in marriage."

CHAPTER 34

Tristram sails to Ireland.

Now Tristram had understood the purpose of what they said before the king. They had persuaded him through their urging that he should certainly marry, and that he should marry no one else but Ísönd. He also considered the fact that his uncle had no heir who might rule after his death, and he realized that, if he refused to undertake the journey, he would give them grounds to suspect and believe that he wanted the king to have no other heir than himself. And when he saw through all their deceit, guile, and cunning, he addressed the king sensibly and calmly.

"Lord king," he said, "consider well the conditions of this journey which you have appointed me to undertake. I am acquainted with Ireland and the customs of the Irish. I know the king and all of his finest nobles, as well as the queen and Princess Ísönd. But I slew the queen's brother, and if I sail to Ireland to ask for the hand of the maiden, and they discover who I am, they will never let me return alive. But in order not to gain enmity from you or from others, and because I desire that my uncle should have a rightful heir, I shall gladly undertake the voyage to further the fame of my kinsman, and to carry out whatever God will permit to the utmost of my power and ability. I shall indeed journey to Ireland to carry out this mission, and if I cannot win Ísönd, I shall not return."

Soon thereafter Tristram made preparations for his voyage. He chose from the king's followers twenty men to accompany him whom he knew to be the most courageous, handsome, and brave in the royal retinue, with the best weapons and good horses. They boarded the ship, supplied with ample provisions and good drink and sufficient money, and loaded the ship with good wheat, flour and honey, wine and all sorts of fine drinks such as men have need of.

Now the ship was manned, and they sailed away on their mission to the land of the enemy. Tristram did not know whether to sue for the hand of the maiden or to lure her on board craftily and sail away with her. If he sued for her hand, then perhaps the suit would be rejected immediately. But if he abducted her from such a powerful father and kinsmen, he could not foresee what the consequences might be. He discussed this with his companions, but none of them was able to give him an answer or to come to a decision. They lamented their mission and were frightened; they cursed the king's counselors for making such demands of them.

Now as Tristram sailed over the Irish Sea, he was vexed and filled with concern. He considered that their best possibility of success would be for him to lure her on board and sail away with her, for he had now decided that they should represent themselves as merchants and remain there for a long time in order to have a good opportunity to decide how he might best secure her secretly and craftily.

Now they sailed night and day until they cast anchor in the harbor of Dublin. They launched their boat and sent two knights to the king to secure his permission, peace, and protection to sell their wares. When the knights came into the presence of the king, they addressed him with fair words, for they were well acquainted with courtly custom.

CHAPTER 35

Tristram requests the king's permission to sell his cargo.

When the two knights had greeted the king, they said, "We are merchants and travel from country to country with our merchandise to earn money, since we do not know how to do any other kind of work. We loaded our ship in Brittany and intended to sail to Flanders, but when we came out onto the sea, a storm arose against us and tossed us to and fro for a long time until we came to land here. We have also learned now that it is difficult to procure provisions in Ireland, and for that reason we have come here with a heavy cargo. Now if we receive permission from you to sell our wines and victuals in peace, we shall anchor our ship in the harbor and offer our wares for sale. But if that is not your wish, we shall sail to other lands."

The king replied, "I grant you permission to trade here as you like in peace and freedom. No one will make charges against you or treat you wrongly. You shall have a splendid welcome and freedom to leave when you like."

When they had been granted this permission by the king, they thanked him, returned to the ship, brought it into the harbor, and tied it up and tented it over. They ate and drank and played all kinds of board games as long as the day lasted. There was no bargaining or trading, but rather they amused themselves with great joy in courtly conversation with chivalrous knights.

But as soon as they awoke the next morning, they heard men and women on the streets begin to shout and scream. Soon they saw people fleeing down toward the sea to save themselves from the fear and affliction of a dreadful dragon, which lived in that kingdom and was wont to come daily into the city, where it caused great loss of life, killing all it could reach with the fire that it spewed from its mouth. There was no one in the entire kingdom so courageous and bold that he dared confront it. All the knights and townsmen who heard its approach fled down to the sea shore to save themselves.

The king had had it proclaimed throughout his entire kingdom that any knight who was brave enough to slay the dragon should be rewarded with the hand of his daughter in marriage and half his kingdom with all honor for himself and his heirs. The king had also committed this to writing, and had confirmed it by oath in the hearing of all the nobility. Many had undertaken this, but the dragon had killed them all, so that there was no one left so brave and bold that he dared confront or encounter it. Even the most courageous immediately fled to save themselves.

Now when Tristram saw the people fleeing, he asked some of the Irish what was wrong and why they were running. They told him the news, about both the dragon and what the king had promised to anyone who might slay the dragon. He thereupon learned with certainty where the dragon remained during the night and at what time it was accustomed to visit the city. He waited until evening without revealing his plan to anyone. Then he told the skipper to have his horse, his saddle, and his armor brought. As day dawned, he put on his full armor.

CHAPTER 36

Tristram slays the dragon.

The dragon kept its custom of visiting the city at dawn. When Tristram least expected it, he heard the shouting. He sprang on his horse so quickly that no one caught sight of him except his shield-bearer. Tristram spurred his horse and hastened as quickly as possible up onto the cliff where the dragon stayed during the night. As he rode thus, he was met by a great number of knights in full armor fleeing from the dragon on swift horses. They quickly shouted to him, begging him to turn back as quickly as possible so as not to be killed by the dragon, which was full of fire and venom. But he did not want to turn back under any circumstances because of their pleas, for he wanted to prove his valor. He peered ahead of him and espied the dragon, which came crawling along, its head held aloft, darting out its eyes and tongue and spewing fire and venom from itself in all directions, so that any living thing that chanced to come near it was rent and killed by the fire.

As soon as the dragon saw Tristram, it roared with rage. Tristram quickly mustered all his courage to test his mettle. He struck his horse with his spurs and thrust his lance forward with such fearful force and fury into the dragon's mouth that all of its teeth that the spear struck flew far out of its head. The iron lance head ran right through the heart and came out through the belly, so that Tristram buried part of the shaft in his neck and body. But the fire that the dragon flung out killed and dispatched his horse. Tristram nimbly sprang from its back, drew his sword, made at the dragon and cut it asunder at the middle.

When the dragon lay dead, he went to its head and cut the tongue out of its skull and stuck it in his war-hose. Then he went back along the path, for he did not want anyone to see him there. Then he noticed a lake which was situated in the valley by a certain wood, and he turned toward it at once. When he had come quite close to the lake, the dragon's tongue in his war-hose became hot, and he inhaled the fumes from the tongue. This poisoned his entire body and deprived him at once of his speech. He fell into a swoon, and his body turned black and blue and swollen, and he lay in this condition, wretched and powerless from the venom, so that he could not stand up, nor could he be helped unless he enjoyed the benefit of someone else's mercy.

CHAPTER 37

About the steward and his deception.

The king had a steward who was an exceedingly arrogant and ambitious man. He was Irish by birth, malicious, fraudulent, and crafty, a liar and a deceiver. He declared that he loved Princess Ísönd, and every day he put on his armor to confront the dragon because of his love for her. But each time he saw the dragon he raced his horse away as speedily as possible, so frightened and faint hearted that if he had been offered all the gold of Ireland at that time, he would not have dared to look back at the eyes of the dragon.

When Tristram attacked the dragon, this steward was watching, fully armed and with drawn sword, but he dared go nowhere near so as not to endanger himself until he felt certain that the dragon was dead. But when he found Tristram nowhere, although his sword and shield and dead horse lay there, he assumed that the dragon had killed the horse and devoured Tristram. He took the bloody sword which lay there, and struck off the dragon's head with his own sword, so that it should redound to his honor that he had in truth slain the dragon.

Then he came galloping his horse through the city and crying in a loud voice, saying, "I have slain the dragon! I have slain the dragon! Now, O, king, I have freed your kingdom and avenged your people and your losses. Pay me my reward at once, and that is your daughter Ísönd. That is in truth my stipulated reward unless you have deceived me with your promise."

When the king heard what the steward claimed to have done and what he demanded, he replied, "I shall convene my counselors this evening and inform you of our decision early tomorrow morning. I shall hold to everything I have stipulated."

When these tidings became known, that the princess had been given, people soon came to her apartment; and when she had ascertained this, she grew fearful and sorrowful, for she hated none of the fiends of hell as she did this steward who claimed to love her. She could not have loved him if she had been given all the world's wealth as a bridal gift.

Then she spoke to her mother. "Never," she said, "will I agree to this, if my father intends to marry me to that wretched man. Never will God wish me such evil as that I should have him as a husband. Rather than come into the power of that deceitful and deedless man, I shall take a knife and kill myself. Where could he ever gain daring and doughtiness, bravery and boldness, he who has always been afraid and fearful among fearless fighters? How could he have killed that dreadful dragon, when everyone in this country knows that he has been damned for his dastardliness and has never proven himself? Never will I be able to believe that he has slain the dragon, nor even that he dared look behind him at the dragon while it was still alive. Rather, he spread this lie about because he wants to possess me. Mother," she continued, "let us go and examine the dragon and look around to see if we can discover who killed it and when it was killed, for someone among these people must be able to tell us something about it."

Then the queen said, "Gladly, daughter, just as you wish."

They now made ready and left the castle by means of a certain secret door that opened out on the orchard. Then they went along the narrow path that led from the orchard out onto the fields, and they found the dragon lying there dead and the horse before him in the sand—the horse all singed and swollen, so that it was the greatest wonder.

"Our Lord knows," said Ísönd, "that the steward never owned this horse. The knight to whom this horse belongs is the one who slew the dragon, wherever he may have gotten to now."

Soon afterward they espied the shield, gilded with the purest gold and with the likeness of a lion traced on it.

CHAPTER 38

Ísönd and Ísodd find Tristram.

"By my faith, mother," said Ísönd, "the steward never carried this shield, for it was just recently made and is gilded both inside and out. It isn't made in the manner of this country. The trusty knight who carried it took vengeance on the dragon for our grief, and our evil steward is now boldly demanding the reward for someone else's deed. He has probably murdered him."

Then they went further and searched all around until they saw where Tristram was lying. And when they found him, they saw that he was black and swollen. They knew then that he had been poisoned, and they found this distressing. The queen wept because of his perilous condition. She touched him with her hand and felt that he was alive and warm. Then she took an herb out of her satchel that we call poison remedy and put it in his mouth between his teeth with some theriaca, and at once he was completely purged of the power of the poison. The faintness fell from his heart; he opened his eyes and his mouth and spoke at once. "O, Lord, my God," he said, "never before have I had such oppressive feelings. Who are you," he asked, "and where have I gotten to?"

"Have no fear. This illness will not harm you, God willing. You will quickly recover from this sickness."

The queen's attendants carried him away so secretly that no one else noticed or knew about it. When they had brought him into the queen's apartment, they removed his armor and found the dragon's tongue in his war-hose. Thereupon the queen prepared a healing ointment to draw the venom out of him. She laid such a potent poultice around his body to draw the poison out of it, and treated him internally with such powerful medicines, that he could feel his whole body being comforted. He had no physician but the queen, and no page except Princess Ísönd, who served him graciously. Tristram often thanked them for their manifold endeavor and kindness, which had brought him relief and rescue from the poison in his body.

Early in the morning the steward came to the royal palace. He carried the dragon's head in his hands and went before the king and spoke in a loud voice. "King," he said, "give ear to my words. You had it trumpeted about and proclaimed before all the people that whoever slew the dragon should receive your daughter in marriage. Now I request that you keep your word and royal oath to me. Have your gift brought forth and marry your daughter to me. Here you can see the head of the dragon, which I have struck off with my sword!"

Then the king replied, "Truly my word shall be kept." Thereupon he called two knights to him and said to them, "Go to the queen's quarters and ask her and my lovely daughter, Princess Ísönd, to come to me."

When the knights arrived there, they delivered the king's message as they had been instructed. Princess Ísönd said that she could not possibly do so, for her head and all her limbs gave her such severe pain that she could find neither rest nor repose anywhere. She requested the king for the sake of her honor that she might have peace and quiet that day, for she could under no circumstances go to him. The queen then arose and went with the knights to the king. With the aid of their counselors the king and queen postponed making a decision and fixed a day for a meeting with the steward.

CHAPTER 39

Queen Ísodd and Tristram converse.

Soon after this day had been appointed for the steward, the vassals returned to their homes.

Now Tristram's companions looked for him everywhere—in fields and woods, roads and forests—and they sadly lamented their distress at his disappearance. They did not know what they should undertake, nor what decision to make, whether to remain or return, because they did not know what had become of him. But he was well cared for in the queen's apartment in the castle, where the queen and Ísönd had healed him so that he had again regained his strength and health.

The queen spoke to Tristram. "Friend," she said, "who are you, and where are you from, and how did you slay the dragon? You much resemble Tantris, who formerly enjoyed great fame here. You must be a blood kinsman of his. And of what rank are you?"

Tristram told the queen what seemed best to him concerning the families of both of them.

"Your majesty," he said, "I am a native of Flanders, and I came here on a merchant voyage. We anchored our ship in the harbor with the king's permission after he had granted us good welcome and peaceful sojourn. One day I armed myself, as other knights did, and rode out in search of the huge serpent, which I had heard was inflicting harm on all your people. I wished to prove my courage and knighthood against the fearful dragon. It so happened, as God willed, that I slew it. I cut its tongue out of its head and stuck it into my war-hose. But then I grew hot from the poison, my whole body became swollen so that I thought I would die, and I went down to the lake. At that moment I fell into such a deep swoon that I do not know who found me. God grant that I may thank whoever came to my aid. I shall always be obligated to render them such good services as I am capable of."

Then the queen spoke. "Friend," she said, "it was I who found you, and I had you brought here secretly. I drew the poison out of your body, and now you will soon recover. If you wish to reward us well for our efforts, then do what is fitting for a wise and noble knight and prudent gentleman. We shall now tell you, friend, what we wish to have as a reward, and if you are the fine fellow we think you are, you will be of great help to us. Our steward has told the king that he slew the dragon, and he demands my daughter Ísönd as a reward and also half of our country and kingdom. The king intends to marry her to him, but she will never consent because he is foolish and full of arrogance, cruel and vicious, as fickle as a harlot, who is faithful to no one, treacherous and envious, hated and cowardly, and afflicted with many other faults that it does not beseem a brave man to have. For this reason Princess Ísönd would rather take her own life than consent to marry him, for her gentility cannot endure being together with his manifold wickedness even though he were to give her whatever she wished to possess in the whole world. And now we have set the day on which the steward is to receive her unless we can prove against him that he did not kill the dragon, and you know for certain that he is not the slayer of the serpent. Now if you will undertake to defend the maiden and the entire kingdom against him, you will be doing us great honor and a worthy service and affection, and you will become famous throughout our whole land because of your kindness and courage. And besides, you will be able to win the maiden and a great realm, for the king will have to give the maiden to you in marriage with all the honor that has been stipulated."

Then Tristram replied. "God knows," he said, "that because of my affection for you I shall prove that he has lied, that he never killed the dragon, and that his hands were nowhere near when I slew it. If he wishes to fight about it, I shall defend Princess Ísönd against him. He shall never have her because he claims her with falseness, falsehoods, and folly. You would have saved my life to no avail if I refused to serve and support you in such obvious hardship and true need. Now, my lady, if it please you and if you have no objections, I should like to summon my shield-bearer, for I should like to have news of my companions and comrades of our merchant voyage. I know that they are distressed because they do not know what has become of me or whether I am dead or alive. I know that they have sought and searched for me and are not certain whether I am living or dead."

The queen replied, "I shall gladly grant this if it is your wish."

Then she sent one of her most trusted pages to bring Tristram's shield-bearer to him, for he wished to talk to him about his own and his companions' needs and about his present condition.

CHAPTER 40

Tristram's companions ride to court.

Now Tristram spoke with his shield-bearer and told him to inform his comrades about his good fortune and about everything that had happened since he had left them and that he was being treated with honor and affection by the queen and Princess Ísönd. The shield-bearer went down to the shore and told these tidings first of all to their captain. The captain informed the knights that Tristram had slain the dragon and about the stipulation that had been made regarding the maiden, the king's daughter, and half the realm of the Irish king. Now they were all comforted and they took heart and rejoiced greatly, and it seemed to them that their circumstances were excellent, since they knew that he was alive. They sold their wine and thanked all the townspeople with warm friendship—so great was their joy over the tidings they had received about Tristram—and they gave the best bargains in wine and foods, honey, flour and wheat, and earned everyone's friendship and the good will of all and pleasing affection.

Now Ísönd took great pains to please Tristram and to provide him with all kinds of foods such as the body needs for strength and vigor until the king of the Irish summoned his retainers, the nobles and vassals throughout the entire kingdom, for he intended to give his daughter in marriage to the steward in order to keep his promise.

Tristram sent word to his companions that they should come to court with the king's vassals. They dressed at once in garments of velvet. Their cloaks were all of exactly the same color, but their garments underneath were of many colors and included white furs and sable and costly fabrics, made with great skill, so that they could not have been better clad if each one of them had been the noblest king of a great realm. Thus attired they mounted their horses, which had gilded saddles, and then rode, two abreast, to the royal palace and dismounted before the royal hall. Their horses, which were well fed and well tried in sharp skirmishes, stamped their feet and neighed so that they could be heard throughout the entire palace. Tristram's men were most handsome and brave in battle. They entered the hall and courteously took their places with a gracious greeting among the greatest vassals on the highest bench. They were mighty men and splendidly arrayed. Then the Irish said among themselves that these men from Flanders were a handsome group, and that a body of Flemish knights must be of great grandeur if these men were merchants from there, "for our men are not of such gallant bearing as they are."

CHAPTER 41

More about the steward and his machinations.

As soon as all were seated, the queen was courteously conducted into the hall with proper dignity and seated beside the king. She was followed by Tristram—handsome, keen-eyed, and grandly attired, who sat down next to Princess Ísönd. All who saw him wondered who he was, for they knew that he was not Irish, and each asked the other, but no one was able to say who he was.

In that great multitude of nobles and vassals who had assembled there, the steward hurriedly sprang to his feet, and bristling and blowing himself up, spoke to the king in a loud voice. "King," he said, "give heed to the task before us today since you have summoned me here. It beseems you to keep the stipulation you made to me, that he who slew the dragon was to receive your daughter and half your kingdom. I am a man of great valor and chivalry. Before a large company of your knights I slew the dragon and cut off its head with one stroke of my sword, as you may see since I have brought the head with me. Now since I slew it, I request that your majesties give me the maiden. But if you will not honor the stipulation, I am prepared to defend my claim and to secure my rights against anyone who tries to withhold them or deprive me of them in accordance with the judgment of the court and the decision of wise men."

"By my faith," said Princess Ísönd, "that boorish braggard wants to be paid and rewarded for his work. It behooves him to earn it in some other manner, otherwise he will never be worthy of the reward. No knight who claims the achievement of another for himself or assumes the bravery of another knows what he is about. You encountered far too little resistance from the dragon for you to get possession of me and a large realm for nothing at all. It seems to me that you must exert yourself more to win my hand and such a great realm than to show us the head of the dragon, for it did not require much effort to carry it into the royal palace. Many a man would long ago have brought the serpent's head to this place if he might so lightly and with so little labor have won my hand as you thought to do when you chanced to chop the head off the dragon. If it be God's will, you will never purchase me for such a petty price."

The steward replied, "Princess Ísönd, why do you want to oppose me and speak so vehemently to me? Now let the king answer first, who will give us a better answer and answer more sensibly. He will surely do as I wish, in regard to both you and his kingdom, as is seemly for him. But you are not behaving as it behooves you, for you never want to love those who love you. That is the way of most women—they always heap abuse and reproach on those who love them and show friendship to their enemies. A woman always hates a man who is fond of her and desires what she cannot have. She seeks what she cannot attain and rejects those whom it beseems her to love. Since I have loved and esteemed you for such a long time, all your desire turns away from me, and in addition you do all you can to impugn my honor, which I gained through my manliness and courageous knighthood, in order to deny and deprive me of what is mine. In truth, when I slew the dragon, you would not have dared be present for all the wealth of this kingdom. You would have been so frightened that you would have lost your mind to see the fierce fight and terrible battle when I overcame the dragon and defeated it."

Princess Ísönd replied. "That is true," she said. "I would surely not have dared for all the gold and jewels in this kingdom to watch you kill the dragon. And I would be a very miserable creature if I desired everything I can have, or if I cared for all those who want to love me. But you do not know my nature when you say that I reject what I really want to have. I want, yet do not always eat my food, for I want some but not all of it. I eat that part of my food that beseems me, but not that part that deceives and disgraces me. You want to have me, but I will never have you for any royal gift whatsoever. You shall never have me for the sake of any services which you have already performed, but for the sake of the great wisdom and accomplishments you boast of, you shall be given the gift you deserve. There are people here in the royal palace who say that someone else and not you slew the dragon, and that you plotted to take the reward that someone else deserves. But you will never live to see that day or enjoy that reward."

The steward said, "Tell me now, where are those persons who speak thus? For there is no one in the king's realm who can say more truthfully than I that he has slain the dragon. And if there is anyone who wants to say otherwise, I shall confront him with weapons and prove in combat that what he maintains is false."

CHAPTER 42

Tristram confronts the steward.

Tristram had listened to Ísönd's words, and when he found that she no longer wished to reply to the steward, he boldly began to speak and said with confident words before all the nobles and court retainers: "Listen, steward! You claimed to have slain the dragon because you struck off its head. But in truth it will be proven that someone else was there before you. This I am prepared to do. If you dare contradict, then you must defend yourself, if you have the courage, and it will then be shown whether you are truthful. It will be proven that it was I who slew the dragon and that you wrongly crave the royal reward. This I am ready to defend with my weapons against your false assertions according to how the king will decide, and his court will stipulate and the wisest men judge."

The king said, "Confirm your duel by a handclasp. Exchange hostages and sureties in order that what is now to be decided will be kept."

Then Tristram gave the king his glove as a pledge, and the king said, "I shall vouch for him, and the Flemish merchants, his companions, will quickly ransom him."

Thereupon Tristram's twenty comrades leaped to their feet, each one of them a most valiant, gallant, and well-armed knight, and spoke. "Your majesty," they said, "we shall be hostages for our comrade, and all our wealth and wares will be his warrant."

Then the king said to the queen, "Lady, I commend this man to your care and keeping. If he fails or lacks the courage to keep his pledge, I shall have you beheaded, for he shall indeed uphold this cause."

The queen replied, "I shall watch over him as worthily as beseems me in our apartment with God's care and seemly hospitality and secure peace, so that no one will dare to offend him."

Now both made pledges and gave hostages and established the day for the duel. But Tristram remained in the queen's quarters, where he was given baths and medical treatment and was carefully guarded and nobly attended and granted everything he requested.

CHAPTER 43

Tristram is revealed as Mórold's slayer.

One day as Tristram sat in his bath, which had been carefully prepared for him with medicinal herbs to draw the pains from his entire body, Princess Ísönd came there to talk with him. She looked at his handsome face with affectionate eyes and said meditatively, "If this man has courage to equal his size, then it is to be hoped that he can defend himself against one man, and if, as seems likely, he has the power to fight a hard fight, for he is of knightly stature."

Thereupon she went to his weapons and looked at them. When she saw his war-hose and coat of mail she said, "This is excellent armor, and this helmet will not break." Then she went to the sword and grasped the hilt and said, "This is a long sword, and if a warrior wields it, it will inflict a death blow on whomever it strikes. All these things provide good armor for those who bargain and barter peacefully, and the sword is a most splendid one unless its steel should fail or have been ruined by the venom of the dragon."

And since Ísönd was curious to see the sword, she drew it from its scabbard, and she at once noticed the notch which had been made when Tristram slew Mórold. Many things came into her mind—that the notch might have been made in the sword on that occasion, and it seemed to her that it could not have been made when the dragon was slain, but that it had been there for a long time. She went to her coffer and took the sword fragment that she had kept and placed it in the notch, and it fit as perfectly into the sword just as though it had sprung out of it. When she saw how neatly the notch fit into the sword, she was distressed from the bottom of her heart. She began at once to tremble with rage and fury, and she broke out in a sweat all over from the hatred and ill will that disturbed and distressed her.

"This scoundrel," she said, "has slain my mother's brother. If I do not kill him with this sword, I am evil and worthless—unless I take his life and rejoice in his death."

She went at once with drawn sword to where Tristram sat in his bath, and quickly raising the sword above her head, said to him, "You evil churl! You must die for the sake of my uncle, whom you dared to kill. No one will believe you now, even though you have disguised yourself for a long time. Now straightway you will die on the spot, and I will kill you with this sword. Nothing can help you now,"—and she brandished the sword again.

But Tristram immediately sprang toward the princess and cried, "Mercy, mercy! Let me speak three words before you kill me. Then do as you please. You have twice given me life and rescued me from double death. Therefore you may slay me without sinning. First you healed me when death seemed certain—that wound I received from a poisoned sword—when I taught you to play the harp. Now you have given me life a second time. Now it is in your power to slay me in this bath, but I am your hostage and appointed to fight to defend your honor, and it is neither womanly nor genteel, neither glorious nor generous to kill me. Gentle and kindhearted maiden, to what purpose will you have healed me, if you wish to kill me now that I am hale and healthy? All your efforts on my behalf will be lost as soon as you see me die, and you will have no more friends then than you have now. Lovely Ísönd, consider that I am pledged to your father and entrusted to you and your mother as a hostage. If you kill me, your mother will have to recompense the king for me in the manner stipulated by him."

When Ísönd heard him mention the day appointed for the duel, which he had established for the steward, she considered that she hated the steward, who wanted to compel her to marry him, more than any other living man, and she looked at Tristram, who was to defend her, and she let the sword sink and did not want to strike him. She wept bitterly and sighed from the bottom of her heart, very angry and in a wrathful mood. But her womanly nature held the sword in check and spared him. When-

ever she grew angry, she brandished the sword; but when she thought of
the steward, her anger vanished.

CHAPTER 44

Tristram presents King Markis's suit for the hand of Princess Ísönd.

Just then Queen Ísodd entered. When she saw her daughter with the
sword in her hand, she said, "Have you lost your wits? What do you
accuse the merchant of?" And she quickly seized her arm and took the
sword from her.

Then Princess Ísönd said, "Oho, mother, this is the man that killed
your brother Mórold."

When the mother comprehended what the maiden had said, she quickly
leaped at Tristram, intending to strike him. But the Princess Ísönd immediately sprang forward and restrained her.

The queen said, "Leave at once! I am going to avenge my brother."

Princess Ísönd said, "Lend me the sword! I will avenge Mórold, for I
am better able than you to kill him without reproach. He is your hostage,
entrusted to your care and safekeeping. You promised to return him to
the king safe and sound. Therefore it does not beseem you to kill him."

Then each one hindered the other so that the queen could not avenge
her brother. Neither of them would let go of the sword, and therefore
vengeance was hampered and delayed.

Tristram was afraid, and he begged for mercy and that his life be spared.
"Queen," he said, "have mercy on me." He spoke so much and with such
meekness and fair words, repeatedly begging for mercy, that finally
neither of them desired to kill him.

Then they sent for the king. And when he arrived, the two women fell
down at his feet. "Sire," they said, "grant us a request that we wish to
ask of you."

"Gladly," said the king, "if it beseems me to accede to it."

"This man," said the queen, "who has come here is Tristram, who slew my brother. But now he has also slain the dragon. I beseech you to forgive the death of Mórold with the stipulation that he free our kingdom and our daughter from the molestation and wrongs of the steward as he has promised us."

Then the king said, "Since I have already promised to grant your request—and you have lost more than I—and since you both wish to forgive him for the death of Mórold—no one has lost more through this than you—I wish to act in this matter as pleases you best."

Then Tristram fell to the feet of the king and thanked him, but Princess Ísönd and the queen raised him up. Then he said to the king, "Hear me, my lord and king! Generous and powerful King Markis of England sends you his message requesting that you give him your daughter Princess Ísönd to wife. And if you desire to know the truth and to agree to a settlement on these conditions, she shall receive as a wedding gift all of Cornwall and authority over all England. There is no better land, nor are there more chivalrous men, in the whole world. Earls and vassals shall be subject to her, and then she will be queen of England. This peace treaty will redound to your honor because it will bring peace and happiness to both kingdoms, England and Ireland."

When the king had heard this message, he said to Tristram, "Swear to me now that this agreement will be kept. I desire also that your companions do likewise, so that there is no treachery at the bottom of it. Then I shall send my daughter, Princess Ísönd, along with you to your uncle, the king."

Then the king had holy relics brought, and Tristram swore an oath that the agreement would be kept on the part of the king of England.

CHAPTER 45

The steward suffers disgrace.

Now the appointed day arrived which had been arranged for the earls and vassals of the royal retinue to see the duel which Tristram and the steward had agreed upon. Then the king conducted Tristram into the hall and spoke in the hearing of all: "Now you are all witnesses that I have faithfully cared for my hostage, and now let him approach, as has been determined and decided."

Then Tristram spoke to the steward before all the nobles and vassals of the king.

"Listen to me, churl!" he said. "I cut this tongue, which I hold here, from the head that lies there when I slew the dragon. It can still be seen in the head where I took out the tongue, and that proves publicly that I did not tell lies or speak foolishly in the presence of many nobles. If you do not believe me, take the head in your hands and see what has been done to the mouth. But if he will not admit that he has lied, let him fetch his armor and prepare to defend himself, for I shall certainly repay him for the lie and prove that he never slew the dragon."

The king had the dragon head carried to him, and then all saw that the tongue had been cut out. Then everyone scorned and scoffed at the steward, and he was buffeted about and harassed and disgraced ever after for having dared to bring forth such a monstrous lie before the nobles and sages of the country. And while the nobles were still assembled in the royal palace, the king announced to all the Irish the decision he had made regarding his daughter—that he had promised her in marriage to the king of England. And that seemed to all present to be a most honorable decision, so that hatred and hostility might be laid aside and peace and freedom be established and maintained between Ireland and Cornwall.

CHAPTER 46

Queen Ísodd prepares a love potion.

Soon thereafter lavish preparations were made for the voyage of the maiden and Tristram. The queen prepared a secret potion with minute care and cunning craft from many kinds of blossoms and grasses, and made it so love-exciting that no living man who drank of it could refrain from loving the woman who drank of it with him as long as he lived. Then the queen poured this potion into a flasket and said to the maiden who was to be Princess Ísönd's attendant and whose name was Bringvet, "Bringvet, guard this flasket well. You shall accompany my daughter. And on the first night when she and the king lie together and he demands wine, give this potion to both of them together."

Bringvet replied, "Gladly, my lady, as you instruct."

After this they went to the ship, fully prepared for the voyage. The king and queen accompanied their daughter to the ship. The tide had come into the river. Then many, men and women, who had been born in that region, wept because of her departure, for she was blessed with friends and dear to every one of them because of her modesty and gentleness.

When Princess Ísönd had come aboard, the sail was hoisted and they put straight out to sea with a favorable wind. But the maiden wept and lamented that she had lost kinsmen and friends and her native land and the tender affection of her father and mother for the sake of strange people, and she disliked such an exchange, and she sighed from the bottom of her heart, saying, "Much rather would I be dead than to have come here." But Tristram consoled her with great tenderness.

Now Tristram sailed on and the weather was fair. But because the heat was oppressive, he became very thirsty and asked for wine to drink. One of his servant lads sprang up at once and filled a cup from the flasket which the queen had given Bringvet for safekeeping. As soon as Tristram received the cup, he drank half of it, and then let Ísönd drink what was left in the cup. And now they were both deceived by the potion they had drunk, for the lad had taken the potion by mistake, and thus he caused for both of them a life filled with grief and enduring distress, with carnal desire and constant longing. At once Tristram's heart turned to Ísönd, and her heart completely to him with such ardent love that they had no means with which to resist it.

They continued to sail with swelling sail on a due course for England. Before long the knights called out that they saw land rising up from the sea. All were pleased at this except Tristram, who was so enamored that if he had had his wish, they would never have seen land, but rather, he would have sailed out on the sea with his love, his pleasure, and his delight. Nevertheless they sailed to land and anchored in a good harbor. People recognized Tristram's ship, and a young man leaped on a fast horse and rode as swiftly as possible to the king. He found him hunting in a forest and addressed him. "Sire," he said, "we saw Tristram's ship landing in the harbor."

When the king heard this news, he was so very happy and joyful that he immediately made the young man a knight and gave him a good suit of armor because of the glad tidings. Then the king rode down to the shore and sent messages throughout his kingdom and celebrated his marriage to Ísönd with great pomp and royal splendor, and he enjoyed himself that day with great happiness, as did all who were present.

Lady Ísönd was a very clever woman. When it had grown late in the evening, she took Tristram by the hand and both of them went together into the king's bedchamber and called Bringvet, her attendant, to them for a private talk. Then Ísönd began to weep bitterly and she asked Bringvet with fair words to help her that night by taking her place in the king's quarters and in his bed as though she were the queen herself, and she would don Bringvet's attire. For she knew that Bringvet was an untouched maiden, as she knew herself was not. They both begged the maiden so long with fair and friendly words that she acceded to their request. She then attired herself completely in the queen's garments and took her lady's place in the king's bed, and the queen wore Bringvet's clothing.

The king was merry and cheerful and rather drunk when he went to bed, and Tristram immediately extinguished the candles of all the candelabra. The king took Bringvet in his arms and had his pleasure with her. But Ísönd was sad and feared that Bringvet would betray her and reveal to the king what had happened. For this reason she remained as close as possible to them during the night to ascertain what they said.

When the king had fallen asleep, Bringvet went away and the queen lay down beside the king. And when he awoke, he demanded wine to drink, and Bringvet cleverly gave him some of the wine that the queen had mixed in Ireland. But the queen did not drink any that time. After a while the king turned to her and slept with her and he did not notice that she was not the same one. And since he found her to be most in-

*Scenes from an ivory or bone jewel casket made in Cologne about 1200: above,
Tristram fights Mórold; below, Bringvet brings the potion to King Markis and
Ísönd.*

Chertsey tiles, ca. 1270: above left, King Markis visits the wounded Tristam; below left, Tristram teaches Ísönd to play the harp; above, Ísönd voyages to heal Tristram.

Early fourteenth-century embroidery from a nunnery in Weinhausen, Hanover, depicting scenes from the Tristram story.

dulgent and pleasing, he showed her much love and such great joy and gentleness that Ísönd became very happy. They talked about all kinds of delightful things, as befitted their youth, with kingly diversion and queenly joy.

Ísönd became cheerful and gentle, the king was affectionate, and she was liked and esteemed by all, rich and poor alike. She and Tristram were together secretly whenever possible, and since she was constantly in his care, it never occurred to anyone to harbor suspicion against them.

CHAPTER 47

The queen plans to have Bringvet killed.

One day when the queen was sitting in her room attired in her finest apparel it occurred to her that no living person knew about her relationship with Tristram except Bringvet alone, her attendant. As she thought about this, she began to suspect that Bringvet might not be willing to remain true to her in this secret affair, but would break her word and tell the king about it, and that ill will would cause her to reveal it. And if it so happened that on some occasion or other she betrayed their love, Ísönd knew that she would be defamed and Tristram would be disgraced and hated. She then considered that, if Bringvet were dead, she would then not need to fear that anyone would disclose it.

She called two of the king's thralls to her and said to them: "Take this girl and lead her out into the forest and strike off her head, and do it so secretly that no one will know about it but me. In truth I pledge to you my word of honor that tomorrow I shall give you your freedom and so much money that you will always be able to live a seemly life."

The thralls replied, "Gladly, my lady," and gave her their pledge upon it.

Thereupon she had her attendant Bringvet summoned and spoke with her. "My most beautiful friend," she said, "I suffer such pain in my head because of the heaviness of my heart, and I have become so ill. Go into the forest with these lads. They know where there are all kinds of herbs. Bring me such as you know I am accustomed to use for poultices with which I draw poison out of people's limbs and alleviate the pain of the heaviness of heart. These two lads will accompany you into the forest."

Bringvet replied, "My lady, I shall gladly go, as you say, for your illness grieves me greatly. If it be the will of God, this illness will not harm you."

Now she went along with the thralls until they came to a place in the forest where the foliage was very dense. One thrall walked before her and the other one behind her. Presently the thrall who walked ahead of her drew his sword. Bringvet began to tremble with fear. She screamed as loudly as she could and folded her hands and asked them in God's name to tell her for what misdeed or offense she was to be killed.

The thrall replied, "That shall not be concealed from you. But as soon as you have heard it, I shall strike you dead with this sword. How have you offended Queen Ísönd, so that she would wish this death for you? For it is she who commanded you to be killed."

When Bringvet heard this, she cried, "Mercy, for the love of God! Let me tell you something about that before you kill me. I want to send a message to my lady, Queen Ísönd. But after you have killed me I beg you in God's name to tell her clearly that I have never transgressed against her. When we departed from Ireland, we each had a nightgown made of silk as white as snow. Her mother put her nightgown on her before they parted. Because I was a poor girl, given into the service of strangers, I protected my nightgown as best I could while I was on the ship. But when Ísönd, my lady, came on board, the sun shone so fiercely that she could not bear to wear her skin kirtle because of the heat. And so she used her good nightgown so much, day and night, that it was blackened by her perspiration. Later, when we arrived here and she went to the king's bed as queen and her nightshirt was not so white as she wished in her great need of it, she asked me to lend her my nightgown and I lent it to her. And I know, as God is my witness, that I have never committed an offense against her unless this displeased her so that she wishes my death for this reason. I know of no other ill will, vexation or anger, offenses or sins between us— not ever. Now take her God's greeting and mine, and tell her that I thanked her for the many honors she has bestowed upon me and for the benevolence she has shown me for such a long time, from my childhood to this day. I forgive her now before God for this my death. Strike now as quickly as you wish."

CHAPTER 48

Bringvet escapes death.

When the thralls understood her words and heard her weeping so woe-
fully, and that she had not committed any other transgression against the
queen, they pitied her very much and found no guilt in her. They tied her
to a large tree. Then they caught a large hare and killed it and cut out its
tongue and then returned and came before the queen. She asked them in
private conference what they had accomplished. Then one of them brought
forth the tongue; they showed it to her, and spoke. "My lady," they said,
"we killed her, and have brought the tongue for you."

Queen Ísönd asked what Bringvet had said before she died. The thralls
delivered her greeting to the queen and related to her everything else she
had said.

"Stop," she cried, "you must not speak thus!" And the queen cried out
in a loud voice. "Evil thralls," she said, "why did you kill my attendant?
I shall avenge her death on your bodies and have you torn asunder by
horses or have you burned to death on a pyre if you do not return her to
me safe and unharmed whom I entrusted to you to accompany into the
forest. I promise you by my faith: if you return her to me, I shall give you
both your freedom."

Then one of the thralls said, "Mercy, my lady! Your mind is fickle.
Everything you said yesterday was different when you ordered us to kill
her and promised us our freedom in return. But now you want to kill us
for her sake. And if we had refused to do what you commanded, we should
already be dead."

Then the queen said, "You sons of whores, bring my attendant to me at
once, and you shall be free this very day."

One of the thralls replied. "May God thank you, my lady," he said.
"Your attendant, Bringvet, is still alive. I shall bring her to you safe and
sound."

She permitted one of the thralls to fetch her, but she had the other one
kept under guard.

The one who had gone away immediately released the maiden in the
forest and accompanied her back to the queen's apartment. As soon as
Queen Ísönd caught sight of her, her grief was transformed into consolation.

The queen at once went to receive her and kissed her more than twenty times.

CHAPTER 49

The Irish harpist abducts Ísönd.

Now Queen Ísönd had put her attendant Bringvet to the test and had found her to be discerning and discreet, and the favor and friendship between them was renewed. The queen now had everything that satisfied her bodily desires—the daily consolation of her lover Tristram. The king was kind to her publicly and Tristram privately, for each of them could do as he pleased at court, since Tristram was the queen's chief counselor. All of their plans were executed with such skill, secrecy, and complete concord that no one except Bringvet knew about them—neither about their words or deeds, their joy, their jesting, nor their caressing. They heard no one speak about their love or harbor any suspicion about it, for Tristram served her with great distinction as the king's nephew and this seemed to all to be fitting because of his kinship with the king. But when Tristram and Ísönd were unable to attain their desires, they were distressed. They guarded their love so well that it never lessened for either of them, either privately or publicly.

Tristram was courageous, courtly, and clever and proven in knighthood. One day, when he had gone on a chase, a large and beautifully adorned ship put into port. On this ship was an Irish nobleman, who was the owner of the ship and the leader of all the men on it. This man was very arrogant and ambitious. He rode to the court of King Markis on a handsome and well-caparisoned steed, and under the skirt of his cloak he carried a harp all adorned with gold. He greeted the king and Queen Ísönd. She recognized him at once, for he had long been enamored of her and it was because of her that he had come to the king's court. As soon as the queen recognized him, she told the king at once who he was and where he was from and requested of the king that he treat him with honor and respect. The king did so and permitted him to eat with him and to share his own dish. This man declared that he was a minstrel, and for that reason he let his harp hang as close as possible to him, for he did not want to lay it down under any circumstances for the sake of anyone's friendship or honor.

When the king had finished eating and the table had been removed, the royal retinue grew cheerful and merry. The king then asked in the hearing of the entire court whether the Irish nobleman knew something about harp playing and whether he would be so kind as to favor the king with a harp performance. The Irishman replied that he would entertain no king in foreign countries unless he knew what reward he was to have in return.

The king said, "Entertain us now with an Irish air and in return you shall have whatever you wish."

He agreed to this, drew forth the harp, and strummed an Irish tune that sounded pleasing to all. Then the king asked him to play another melody, just as good or even more pleasing than the first. He played a second melody twice as beautiful as the first, so that it was a joy to listen to it. And then he said to the king, in the hearing of the entire retinue, that the king should keep the agreement which had been made and which the king himself had determined.

"That shall be," said the king. "Tell me what you wish to have."

The Irishman replied, "You shall give me Ísönd, for you have neither wealth nor anything else that I would rather have."

The king replied, "By my faith, you shall never have her. Ask for something that you may receive."

He replied to the king, "Now you are lying and breaking your oath which you made to me in the hearing of all your retainers. It is legal and just that you no longer reign in your realm, for that ruler who publicly prevaricates and repudiates his oath and his word shall never rule or reign over rightful men. But if you refuse what I have requested, I shall refer it to the judgment of reliable men. And if you should find someone who refuses to grant me this and dares to dispute it, I shall defend against him this very day in the presence of your entire court my claim that you agreed to grant me my wish, whatever it might be that I should ask of you. Now if you deny me what you have promised me, you have no right to this realm, and I shall prove this against you with my sword if your retinue will judge justly and these trusty men will prove their loyalty to me."

CHAPTER 50

Tristram rescues Ísönd from the Irish harpist.

King Markis had listened to his words, and he now looked over all the benches at his men, but found no one among his retainers who dared gainsay the Irish nobleman, or to espouse the king's cause, or to rescue the queen, for they all knew that he was a fierce man, bold in battle and accomplished in the use of arms and diverse accomplishments.

When the king perceived that no one was willing to confront the Irishman, he relinquished his wife into his power in accordance with the decision of his counselors and knights. He received her graciously and took her on horseback down to the seashore. Great was her grief as she lamented her predicament, filled with anxiety and weeping and sighing sorrowfully. She cursed the day on which her sweetheart had gone off on the chase, for if he had been there when she was abandoned, he would have redeemed her in fierce combat, and would surely rather have given up his life than not win her back. The Irishman carried her, weeping, into his tent. And when she had been placed on the bed, he ordered that the ship be got ready immediately so that they might sail away as soon as possible. But the ship was completely beached on dry sand, and the tide was just beginning to rise and was still far away from the vessel.

At this moment Tristram returned from the forest, and he was informed of the news that Queen Ísönd had been surrendered and carried away. He called his page, seized his fiddle, sprang on his steed, and galloped swiftly down toward the tents. When he came to a certain slope near the tent, he dismounted and gave his horse to his page to guard. He went with his fiddle as quickly as possible to the tent and saw Ísönd lying in the arms of the nobleman. He was doing his best to console her, but she resisted his consolation, weeping and wailing.

When the Irishman saw the fiddler coming into the tent, he spoke: "Churl," he said, "give us some good entertainment with your fiddle, and I shall give you a cloak and good robe if you can cheer up my lady."

Tristram replied, "May God reward you, sir. I shall accomplish so much that she will not be mournful for half a year if I take it to heart to entertain her."

Then he made ready his fiddle and gave them pleasing entertainment with sweet songs. Ísönd listened during the night and was comforted by her friend's arrival and affection. When he finished his entertainment, the vessel was afloat, and one of the Irishmen spoke to the nobleman. "My lord," he said, "let us depart at once. You are tarrying here far too long. If Sir Tristram returns from the chase, it is to be feared that he will delay our departure somewhat. He is renowned above all the knights in this kingdom, and he is the commander of all of them."

Then the nobleman replied: "Shame on those who in any way fear his attacks. Friend," he said, "play me another tune for the consolation of Ísönd, my lady, so that you overcome her grief."

Tristram tuned his fiddle and began to play a lay of love, especially sweet to hear, and Ísönd listened, completely engrossed in it. The lay he played was long and had a rather sad ending. Meanwhile the tide had risen so high that it was impossible to get to the gangway because of the water, and indeed, the gangway had floated out past the ship.

Then the Irishman said, "What shall we do now? How shall we get Ísönd on board? Let us wait until the tide recedes so that she can reach the bridge with dry feet."

Tristram replied, "I have a good horse in the dale nearby."

"Be so kind," said the Irishman, "as to bring the horse here."

Tristram went at once to his horse and sprang on its back, and taking his sword, he came galloping back to the Irish nobleman.

"Sir," he said, "hand Ísönd up to me. I promise that I shall deal with her properly."

The Irishman lifted her up to the saddle and bade Tristram with fair words to deal fitly and properly with his sweetheart.

When Tristram had received Ísönd, he called out with a loud voice. "Listen," he said, "you heedless and foolish fellow. You won Ísönd with your harp, and now you have lost her because of a fiddle. You deserved to be deprived of her since you won her with deception. Return home to Ireland, dishonored and disgraced, you treacherous traitor. You took her from the king with deception, and I took her from you with deceit."

Thereupon he gave his horse the spurs and rode hurriedly up to the sands and thus into the forest. Now the Irishman had indeed lost Ísönd, for Tristram had taken his beloved away.

While Tristram and Ísönd were in the forest, evening came. They made a shelter as best they could with what materials were at hand and enjoyed a delightful rest there that night. In the morning, when day came, he rode home with her to the king's castle and returned her to the king.

"Sire," he said, "by my faith, it is not very befitting for a woman to love a man who gives her away for a performance on the harp. Guard her better in future, for great cleverness was involved in her return."

CHAPTER 51

Mariadokk discovers the love of Tristram and Ísönd.

Tristram's love for Ísönd was unchanging, and her love for him was constant and faithful. Each loved the other in an equally charming and becoming manner. The strength of their love was so great that they long seemed to have one heart and one mind until people began to talk and wonder about it. Yet there was no one who knew anything with certainty, and such talk was merely a matter of suspicion.

Tristram had a companion whom he loved very much with complete trust and fine comradeship. He was a counselor of the king and so close to him that he could persuade him in whatever he wished, and his name was Maríadokk. They were always together, he and Tristram, and they shared one room. It so happened one night, after they had gone to bed together and the steward had fallen asleep, that Tristram stole away from him. And when he came out, snow had fallen and the moon was shining as brightly as if it were day. When he reached the wooden orchard fence, he pulled away one of the palings at the place where he was accustomed to enter. And Bringvet took him by the hand and led him to Queen Ísönd. She took a basket made of ash wood and placed it upside down over the candlestick so that the light of the candle should not shine upon them. Then she went to bed and forgot to lock the door, and Tristram made love to the queen.

Meanwhile the steward dreamed a dream in which he thought he saw a huge wild boar running from the forest. His snout was wide-open and he gnashed his tusks as though he were in a rage and snarled so dreadfully as though he wanted to slash everything to pieces, and he made for the castle. When he got there, no one in the entire royal retinue dared confront him or go against him or hold his ground before him. And Maríadokk saw him race to the king's bed and slash him between the shoulders so that the blood and froth that ran from his snout soiled all the bedclothes. Many people came to the help of the king, but he dared do nothing against the boar. Then Maríadokk awoke in fatigue and terror from that dream and thought at first that it was true. But then he comprehended that it was a dream, and it seemed marvelous to him and he wondered what it might mean.

Then he called to Tristram, his companion, and wanted to tell him these tidings. He groped about seeking him, and wanted to tell him his dream, but he found him nowhere. He then got up and went to the door and found it open. Thinking that Tristram had gone somewhere to amuse himself that night, Maríadokk thought it strange that he had managed to get out so secretly that no one had been able to notice his departure and also that he had told no one where he intended to go. When he saw his footprints in the snow before him, he put on his shoes and followed his trail, for the moon provided abundant light. When he came to the garden, he at once found the opening through which Tristram had entered. He wondered where he had gotten to—for he had no suspicion concerning the queen, but thought rather that Tristram was fond of the queen's attendant—and he continued on his way and entered secretly and as quietly as possible to try to discover how matters stood. After a while he heard Tristram and the queen conversing. He was uncertain what he should undertake to do. He was greatly distressed in his mind, and it was displeasing to him to tolerate such disgrace and dishonor of the king. Yet he did not dare disclose the matter for fear of slandering them. He returned by the same path that night, and pretended to know nothing about it. When Tristram returned, he lay down in the bed beside him, and neither spoke to the other about it.

This was the first incident concerning their love that was discovered, for never before had anyone noticed anything, either by night or by day. And yet it was a long time before Tristram's enviers and enemies disclosed their secret to King Markis.

Great grief and grievous anguish came to the king because of this, anxiety and unrest, and he did not know what to undertake except to have their doings spied upon.

CHAPTER 52

King Markis makes trial of Queen Ísönd.

The king now considered putting the queen to the test, and in order to bring forth a reply, he told her a falsehood. One night, as the king lay beside her in bed, he spoke to her in words that seemed sad. "My lady," he said, "I intend to become a pilgrim and to fare abroad to visit holy places for the good of my soul. Now I do not know into whose hands I should entrust the custody of my court. Therefore I should like to hear what advice you have to offer or what seems best and most pleasing to you. Give me your advice and tell me in whose keeping you should like to be and I shall follow your counsel."

Ísönd replied, "It seems strange to me that you should be in doubt as to what is best for you to do in the matter you have brought up. Who else should take care of me but Sir Tristram? It seems to me most fitting that I should be in his care. He is able to defend your kingdom and to watch over your court. He is your nephew, and he will put forth every effort to see that your honor is everywhere respected and that your court is faithfully served and devotedly preserved in complete peace and to the contentment of all."

Having heard her words and her counsel, the king, as soon as it was day, went to his counselor who wished the queen evil and told him everything Ísönd had said. He replied, "Then what I have heard said is true. You can clearly perceive from her words that she wants to be where she likes it best, for she loves him so greatly that she cannot conceal it. And it is strange that you are willing to endure such disgrace so long and that you are unwilling to drive Tristram away from you."

But the king was in great bewilderment and uncertainty about it but suspected that what had been told him about Ísönd and Tristram might be true.

Ísönd now arose from her bed, and calling Bringvet, her attendant, to her, said, "My dearest friend, do you know what? I have heard good, pleasing news: the king intends to go abroad and leave me in the care of my beloved. Then we can enjoy our pleasure and comfort each other, no matter who is displeased by it."

Bringvet replied, "How do you know? Who told you this?"

Then Ísönd told her what the king had said.

But Bringvet immediately detected her foolishness and said, "You do not know how to dissemble. The king put you to the test and discovered that you can't disguise your true feelings. It was the counselor who brought it about that you betrayed yourself through the lies you were told and believed. Now they have found it out and proved it with your own words."

And she gave her some instructions and taught her what answers she should give the king and how to protect herself against the falsehoods which the counselor was telling about her.

CHAPTER 53

More about Markis and Ísönd.

With sleeplessness and concern, King Markis greatly desired and endeavored to know with true certainty what it most behooved him to believe about the blame which had fallen on Ísönd and Tristram. The following night, as he lay in bed beside Ísönd, he again resorted to wiles in order to put Ísönd to the test, and he took her into his arms with many caresses and sweet kisses and with that pastime which pleases most people, cotters as well as kings. But she realized immediately that he wished to make trial of her as he had done before. She immediately feigned a complete change of mood, sighing from the bottom of her heart and cursing the day on which she had first seen him and he had taken her into his bed.

"Wretch that I am," she said, "I was born for grief and distress. Everything has always turned out miserably for me. What befits me best can prove to be the worst for me, and what I would most like to have, is least granted to me."

And with much weeping she displayed to the king sorrow and suffering, anxiety and affliction, anger and anguish.

Then the king said to her, "My beautiful lady, what is the matter? Why are you weeping?"

Ísönd replied, "Many are the reasons for my sorrow and unbearable pain, unless you grant me relief. I thought that what you said last night was spoken in jest, and that you were joking when you said you intended to go abroad. But now I have learned the truth about your plans to go away. Wretched is the woman who loves a man too dearly. No woman can trust a man, seeing that you intend to go away and leave me here. But since you have made that decision—why did you conceal it from me? Today I was told for certain that you wish to go away. Where do you intend to leave me, and which friends of ours are to take care of me? It was for your sake that I gave up all means of help—father and mother, friends and family and great honors as well as happiness and my native land. It is a dishonor and a disgrace to you to leave me here. Never will I find consolation, night or day, as long as I am deprived of your love. For the sake of God, remain at home or else let me, grief-stricken, accompany you."

King Markis said, "My lady, I shall not leave you here alone, for Tristram, my nephew, will protect you with great affection and honorable service. No one in my realm do I love so greatly as him, particularly because he serves you so chivalrously."

Ísönd replied, "My misfortune will be complete if Tristram is to protect me and if I am to be in his custody. I understand his service, affection, and gentle disposition toward me. It is all falsehood and sham and flattery. He pretends to be my friend because he killed my uncle, and he speaks sweetly to me so that I won't hate him and take vengeance on him. But he should know for certain that his fawning cannot console me for the deep anguish, disgrace and loss he inflicted on me and my family. If he were not your nephew, my lord, I would long ago have let him feel my wrath and would have avenged my grief and affliction on him. And now I would prefer never to see him or speak to him again. The reason I pretend to be friendly to him is that people slander me and accuse me of hating your kinsman and dearest friend, for it is a well-known saying that women can have terrible dispositions. They do not care for their husbands' relatives and refuse to have them near them night or day in work or speech. Because of this I have protected myself against blame and reproach by accepting his service and his blandishments. Never again shall I be in his power or accept his service, but rather, my lord, I implore you to let me go with you."

So persuasively did she speak on this occasion that the king completely gave up his anger against her. Then he went to the counselor and told him that no love existed between the queen and Tristram. But the counselor sought with all his cleverness to teach the king what he should say to the queen to test her. And when the king had heard his words, he returned to the queen and told her that he did indeed intend to go on a journey and that she should remain in the custody of the most excellent men and friends who would honor her with the greatest favor and esteem,—"and I wish no one to do anything that you dislike or that is displeasing to you. But since it does not please you that my nephew Tristram should be in your service, I shall, because of my affection for you, remove him from your presence and send him abroad, for under no circumstances will I favor him if it is not in accord with your desire and honor."

Ísönd replied, "Sire, never should you do such an evil thing, for then people throughout your entire kingdom would say that I had caused you to design such a plan and that I hate your nephew because of Mórold's death and that I incited you to hate him so that I could deprive him of the benefits of your kingdom, whereas he is obligated first and foremost to protect you. Because of this I would be defamed, and I do not want you to hate your kinsman because of your love for me. It does not beseem you to have him go abroad for my sake, nor to jeopardize the peace and prosperity of your country. For I am only a woman, and if war were to come, your enemies would soon take your country from me, since I lack the strength and power to defend it. And then people would say that I had got rid of Tristram, the most powerful defense of our realm, because I hated him so deeply that he could not stay here because of me. Now do one or the other—let me go with you at once, or else entrust him with the care and defense of your kingdom."

The king listened eagerly to the words of Ísönd, and felt that she harbored a strong feeling of good will toward Tristram, and he pondered the same suspicion, and then he grew sorrowful because of grief and anxiety, and his anger and distress returned anew.

But in the morning the queen went to speak with Bringvet in secret. And Bringvet said she was foolish and lacked understanding, and taught her a good stratagem and how she should reply to the king in regard to his plan to drive Tristram away.

CHAPTER 54

The king has Tristram and Ísönd spied upon.

Thereafter the king no longer wished to have Tristram at court because of the slander that had fallen upon Tristram and the queen, and he had them strictly separated. Tristram now lived in a town at the foot of the castle, where he maintained a dwelling of great elegance. But now he was always sorrowful, as was Ísönd also, because they could not be together. Because they were apart from each other, both of them grew pale from sorrow and sadness, for they had lost all joy. Now the entire court apprehended their affliction, and it became manifest to the king. The king now devised a stratagem, for he knew that they desired to meet since they endured grief and distress from being parted and closely guarded.

One day the king sent for his hunting dogs and had his horses made ready. He sent men out into the forest to erect huts and pitch tents and had wine and food taken there, for he said he planned to devote six weeks or more to the hunt. The king took leave of the queen to pursue this pleasure and rode off into the forest.

When Tristram learned of the king's departure, his heart was completely consoled. He pretended to be ill so that he could remain behind and try to find some expedient whereby he could see the queen. He took a twig and carved from it beautiful chips, so skillfully that no one had ever seen the like, for when they were cast onto the water they did not sink but floated on the surface as though made of foam, and no current could destroy them. Whenever Tristram wished to speak with Ísönd, he cast the chips of wood into the brook which flowed past the tower and in front of the queen's bedroom, and the queen understood at once and knew from this wile his wish for a rendezvous.

As Tristram stood carving the twig, a certain dwarf came walking out of the castle and said, "God's greeting and Lady Ísönd's. She sends you a message that she would like to see you. Now, don't neglect under any circumstances to go to her at the place where you last met her. I am certain that you know and remember the place. I tell this only to you and in secret, and it is not likely that there will soon be another opportunity like this, for the entire court has ridden out on the hunt. That is why the queen sends word to you to come tonight to visit her. Now tell me the message that you want to send to her, for I do not dare remain here any longer on account of those evil persons who are envious of me and who will tell the king that I am the instigator of all the wickedness that goes on between you. If they knew that I am here now, they would defame and denounce me before the king."

Tristram said to him, "Friend, may God bless you for being willing to bring me a message, and you shall have your reward if I live long enough. Now, for the time being, although it is but little, I shall give you my cloak trimmed with white fur, and the next time it will be something better. Now I ask you, please, to tell gentle Ísönd that I send her God's greeting and my friendship, and tell her that I cannot come to her today because I have a dreadful headache and was very ill all night long. But tomorrow, if I possibly can, I shall go to see her if she has need of anything from me. Then she can say whatever she wants to."

The dwarf took leave and returned to the castle, where the king had concealed himself in order to lie in wait for them, and told the king what he had said to Tristram and how he had replied.

"King," he said, "Tristram concealed everything from me. But in truth, tonight you will see and witness the behavior that they have been accustomed to practice so long in secret, for I saw him carving the chips that he is in the habit of throwing into the brook in order to entice and direct Ísönd to him." And they discussed this matter for a long time and finally devised this plan and this scheme: the king should conceal himself during the night and lie in ambush at the place where they were accustomed to meeting.

CHAPTER 55

The evil dwarf and his wiles.

As evening drew near, Tristram made ready and went to the brook near the orchard, for Ísönd was accustomed to going there every evening to sit by the brook for a while for her amusement and to lament the events of her youth. When she arrived there, she saw the wooden chips floating and knew that Tristram had already gone to the orchard. She completely covered herself with her cloak, which was made of white furs, and went into the garden with covered head and toward the trees where the king was already waiting. Tristram had entered from the opposite side through the paling fence, and was approaching the tree by which they were wont to meet. But just then the moon came up and shone beautifully. He caught sight of the king's shadow on the ground and halted immediately, for he knew that the king wanted to spy on them. He was greatly distressed for the sake of the queen and feared that she would fail to notice the shadow. But she soon caught sight of it, and then she was greatly frightened for Tristram's sake. And they both went away. They knew that they had been betrayed in this matter, and they were filled with grief and great anxiety. But the king remained sitting under the tree, and he was still in such great doubt and uncertainty about this matter that he abandoned his anger against both of them.

Then it happened one day that they had themselves bled, the king and the queen and Tristram, for the king still wanted to put them to the test secretly in his sleeping chamber. Tristram was unable to see through the stratagem. During the night, after everyone had gone to bed and the king had let no one but Tristram remain there, he spoke to him.

"Nephew," said the king, "put out all the candles; the light annoys me." The reason he spoke that way was that he had long been cogitating great schemes and tricks at the instigation of the evil dwarf, who was still ill-disposed toward Queen Ísönd and Tristram. The evil dwarf then got out of bed quietly and took a container full of wheat flour, which he had beside his bed, and scattered the flour all over the floor so that Tristram's footprints might be seen in the flour if he went to the queen. But Bringvet soon detected what he had done and informed Tristram.

Presently the king arose in the middle of the night, saying that he was weary of lying in bed. He said he wished to attend matins and told the dwarf to accompany him. When the king had left, and Tristram remained lying there, Tristram began to think about how he could reach the queen, for he knew that if he walked over to her bed, his footprints could be seen in the flour. Therefore he sprang with both feet over the flour and into the queen's bed. The effort of leaping was so strenuous that his veins opened and bled all night. When he got up, he leaped back into his bed again.

Shortly afterward the king returned and saw that there was blood on his bed, and he asked Ísönd where the blood came from. She said that her hand had been bleeding. The king then went to Tristram's bed and saw that it was all bloody. He knew then that Ísönd had lied. This was a clear cause for suspicion, and the king was grieved and angered. He did not know what was true for certain, except for the blood that he saw, and that was neither a true charge nor a clear proof of guilt. Therefore the king was in doubt and did not know what to believe, for he had no reliable evidence through which they could be exculpated. And yet he was not under any circumstance willing to give up; rather, he intended to make the matter public, but without bringing disgrace to them. Therefore he summoned all his vassals and advisers and disclosed to them the vexation he endured because of Ísönd and Tristram. All of them discussed the matter, intent on taking vengeance if true cause were found.

CHAPTER 56

The council meets to discuss the accusations against Tristram and Ísönd.

Shortly thereafter the king summoned all his counselors to London, and all who wished to keep the king's friendship complied, bishops and vassals and all of the wisest men in England. And when they had assembled there, the king asked them to tender him wholesome counsel as to how he could bring to an end this matter concerning Tristram and Ísönd, which had brought such shameful defamation upon him that he was disgraced throughout his entire realm. Then the royal counselors expressed their opinions, some foolishly, but others soundly and sensibly.

Presently an elderly bishop arose and addressed the king. "Sire," he said, "listen to what I have to say, and if it is just, give it your approval. There are many in our country who make accusations against Tristram, but none would dare try to prove them. You seek counsel, Lord King, and it behooves all of us to give you wholesome counsel, trustworthy and true. It does not beseem you to state this defamation publicly, nor can you dishonor them because of it, for you have not apprehended them in such acts as would clearly enable you to prove their guilt. In what manner do

you intend to condemn your nephew and your wife? For you and Ísönd
are lawfully married, and you can under no circumstances divorce her as
matters stand, since there is no clear evidence on which to bring charges
against her for the accusations her enemies and enviers make against her.
Nor does it beseem you to neglect this matter in view of the fact that most
of the people, whether rightly or wrongly, believe and gossip about this
slander and reproach, for people often believe what is wrong no less than
what is right. Now, in view of the slander which you have patiently
endured for such a long time and because of which you have reproached the
queen, it seems fitting that Queen Ísönd should appear before this assembly
of noblemen. Then listen to my words and to her reply. And after she has
made her reply, we shall insist on the basis of a just judgment that she
shall not be permitted to sleep in the king's bed until she has cleared
herself of this slander."

The king replied, "I gladly approve this judgment here before all my
nobles and vassals."

Thereupon they sent for Ísönd, and she came to their assembly in the
hall and sat down. Then the bishop arose and addressed her.

"Queen," he said, "listen to what the king has commanded me to
inform you. All people, both at court and throughout the kingdom, know
about a certain slander that has befallen you and that has persisted
publicly about you and Tristram, our king's kinsman, for better than
twelve months. Whether rightly or wrongly, it is clear that slander and
blame attach to you and disgrace to the king. The king has seen for certain
nothing but good, except for that slander which people spread about you,
but not by reason of a true test or cogent proof. Now, before the nobles
and vassals I charge and demand that you clear yourself and the king of
this doubt and uncertainty, for it is not seemly for you to share the king's
bed with public knowledge until you have cleared yourself of this slander."

Ísönd was prudent and polite, and a most beautiful and eloquent
woman, and she stood before the king and said, "Good king, you may
know for certain that I am well aware of the slander that envious and
malicious men utter concerning me, for it was said long ago that no one
lives without accusation and defamation. It seems strange to me that men
should lie about me when I am innocent. They find this safe and easy to do,
since I am a foreigner, far from friends and kinsmen, alone in a strange land
among strange people, like a captive woman taken as booty, and I know
that for this reason no one will have compassion on me in my perplexity.
Now I request the king, my lord, to have my case judged before the entire
court by means of a proof of innocence. Never can a judgment be made

that is so severe that I should not submit to it to rid myself of the blame of envious men—for I am innocent of their slander—whether this be the bearing of a red-hot iron or some other proof of innocence. And if I fail this trial of my innocence, let the king have me burned to death or torn asunder by horses."

CHAPTER 57

The king is pleased with Ísönd's suggestion.

The king listened to Ísönd's words as she declared that she would gladly undergo the ordeal of the red-hot iron or any other test to prove her innocence, and he knew that it did not behoove him to make further demands of her. Since he possessed neither certain proof nor clear evidence of guilt against her, he had to grant her a just judgment, and he replied to her.

"Come here," he said, "and swear to me before these noblemen that you will undergo the test of innocence and keep the promise you have just made, and we shall gladly agree to it. You, Ísönd, are to journey to Korbinborg, and I summon all of you noblemen to appear there to attend to my honor and my rights. Let us all assemble there one month from today."

Then Ísönd went and pledged to the king that she would undergo the trial of her innocence, as he himself had requested. The nobles and court attendants then withdrew and returned home. But Ísönd remained behind in grief and anxiety, for she knew she was guilty of the charge for which she had been condemned and disgraced.

CHAPTER 58

Tristram carries Ísönd from the ship.

As the appointed day approached, Ísönd devised a plan. Then she sent word to Tristram that he should come to meet her at a certain ford in the river on the day she set for him, and that he should disguise himself as completely as possible. She wanted him to carry her from the ship when she was ferried across the river, and then she would tell him a secret.

Tristram carefully kept his promise that he would be there with Ísönd on the appointed day, and he was so well disguised that no one recognized him. His entire face was stained yellow, and he was dressed in a shabby tunic of homespun, over which he wore an old cloak. The queen approached in a boat from the other side of the river. She beckoned to Tristram at once, and thereupon landed the boat. She called to Tristram in a loud voice.

"Friend," she said, "come here and carry me out of the boat. You look like a good boatsman."

Tristram immediately went to the boat and took her in his arms, and as he was carrying her, she told him in a low voice that he should fall on top of her when they got up on the sandy bank. And when he had walked away from the boat and had come a short distance from the river, she lifted up her dress and he at once fell upon her.

When her men saw that, they came running quickly from the boat— some with poles, some with sticks, and some with oars—and wanted to beat him to death. But the queen said they should do him no harm, for he had not fallen down on purpose, but because he was weak and weary from walking—"for he is a pilgrim and has come from a long journey."

Then they joked at her words and laughed at the manner in which the pilgrim had fallen with her. And all of them thought she was an exceedingly gracious lady, for she was the only one who had not wished him to be harmed. But no one knew why she had devised this stratagem. Thereupon they sprang on their horses and rode on their way, joking and jesting about the pilgrim and his comical mishap.

"Now is it so surprising," said Ísönd, "that the pilgrim wanted to enjoy himself by squeezing my white thighs? But now I can under no circumstances swear an oath that no one else has lain there but the king."

Then they rode to the castle of the king, and there the queen and all her companions dismounted from their horses.

CHAPTER 59

Ísönd takes an oath and carries the red-hot iron.

The members of the king's court had assembled there in large number. The king was now stern and severe, eager and anxious to avenge himself and to put Ísönd to the test with the red-hot iron that she was to carry on account of Tristram. The iron had already been placed in the fire and was in readiness. Three bishops had consecrated it. Then Ísönd heard mass and gave away great and generous gifts of alms. Whatever she possessed in gold and silver, garments and goblets—of this she gave a large share to the poor for the sake of God's love, likewise to the sick and the sore, and to the fatherless and to penniless widows. Then she approached with bare feet, dressed in a woolen garment, and everyone was grieved at her condition. All wept, strangers and acquaintances, foreigners and countrymen, rich and poor, young and old—all of them felt pity for her in their hearts. Then holy relics were brought forth, on which she should swear an oath pleading her innocence. She approached, weeping, and placed her hand on the holy relics. Then she heard the nobles wrangling about her oath formula. Some wanted to constrain and distress her, but some wished to help her in the formulation of the oath. Most of them agreed with the king that the oath formula should be most rigorous.

Then Ísönd spoke. "King," she said, "hear my oath. Never was man born of woman who came close to me naked except you, king, and that poor pilgrim who carried me from the boat and fell upon me in the sight of all of you. May God help me in this trial and purge me with this iron. This I affirm before God and all the saints. Now if I have omitted anything in the framing of this oath, add to it quickly and I shall swear to it."

The king saw Ísönd weep, and many other persons for her sake, rich and poor, because of her grief. Then his heart was deeply touched, and he spoke to Ísönd.

"I have heard," he said, "and it seems to me that nothing need be added. Now take up this red-hot iron, and may God purge you in accordance with your deserts and your oath."

"Yes," she said, and boldly took the iron in her hand and carried it in such a way that no one detected any cowardice or faintheartedness in her. And God in his gentle mercy granted her sweet vindication and reconciliation and concord with the king, her lord and husband, with abundant love, honor, and esteem.

CHAPTER 60

The king is reconciled with the queen.

As soon as Ísönd had proven her innocence through the ordeal of the red-hot iron, she told the king that he had behaved childishly to hate his nephew on account of the queen. Then the king abandoned his foolishness and regretted that he had harbored suspicion against his nephew and inflicted all kinds of grief and distress upon himself needlessly. But now his doubts had been so thoroughly dispelled that his mind was completely cleansed and impervious to suspicion despite all detractors. The king now thought that Ísönd was unscathed by the slander to which she had been subjected, and he was most gentle in consoling her after her grievous affliction. All that he possessed he valued as nothing beside her love and affection. He loved her beyond measure, so that there was no other creature of God that pleased him so well as beautiful Ísönd.

CHAPTER 61

A dog from the realm of the elves.

When Tristram, valiant and splendid man, had departed from the kingdom after he and the king had parted in anger, Tristram for a while served a duke in Poland, who honored and esteemed him above all his friends because of his renown and lineage, his valor and chivalry, his courteous conduct and courtly deportment, and every manner of manliness, which distinguished him above all others.

It happened one day that Tristram was filled with concern, as are those who have come into a strange country. And because he was so far from his solace, love, and delight, he often sighed from the bottom of his heart, pondering the grief and distress that were his because he was so far from the one who comforted him. When the duke discovered this, he ordered his pages to bring them his own special diversion, that he might cheer up Tristram, who was so downcast at his court, and whom he wished to amuse and show some kindness if thereby he might cheer him up.

Presently some of the duke's pages brought a rug made of costly stuff and spread it on the floor before the duke. Then the others returned, leading his pet dog, which had been sent to him from Elfland.

This was such a marvelously beautiful creature that never has a man been born who could relate or record its shape or appearance, for however one looked at the dog, it displayed so many colors that no one could discern or fix them. If one regarded it from the front, it appeared white or black or green on the side which faced one. But if one looked at it from the side, it seemed blood red, as though the flesh side of the hide were turned outward and the hair side inward; sometimes it seemed as though it were colored dark brown, and then immediately afterward as though it had a bright red skin. But those who looked at it lengthwise could least determine what color it was, for it seemed to them to have no color at all as far as people could ascertain. The dog had come from the island called Poland, and had been given to the duke by an elf woman. Never has a living creature so large been more beautiful or agreeable, nor so clever, gentle, and obliging.

The pages brought this dog to the duke, leading it on a golden chain from his treasure house. They took off the chain at once, and as soon as it was free, it shook itself so that the bell fastened to its neck tinkled with such a beautiful sound that all of Tristram's grief disappeared, and he forgot his sweetheart, and his mind, mood, and heart were all so changed that he scarcely knew whether he was himself or someone else. There was no living person, who, hearing the sound of the bell, would not immediately be consoled of his grief from the bottom of his heart and filled with joy and gladness, nor would he wish to have any other entertainment. Tristram listened closely to the sound and looked carefully at the dog, and the color of the dog seemed even more marvelous to him than the tinkling of the bell. He then touched it with his hand and felt that it had a soft and silky fleece. He thought then that he could not go on living if he could not procure this dog for the entertainment of Ísönd, his sweetheart, but he did not know how he could gain possession of it. He did not allow it to be known, however, that he wanted the dog, for the duke had treated him so cordially that he did not, under any condition, wish to forsake him or be without his friendship.

CHAPTER 62

Tristram slays the giant Urgan.

As the story of Tristram truly tells us, there was a certain giant in those days who lived in a district along the seashore. Every twelve months he exacted tribute from the entire country, and this was one-tenth of all the livestock. The duke paid him this tribute each year, and now the giant had come again to collect it. Then it was announced throughout the country by the blowing of trumpets that this tribute was to be paid to the giant Urgan, and all came—vassals, merchants and cotters, townsmen and husbandmen—each according to his wealth, driving their livestock to the giant. It was most astonishing how much livestock there was, and as the people herded their cattle toward the giant, they raised a great hue and cry.

Tristram asked where that great clamor was coming from, and who owned the livestock and who was to have it. The duke quickly explained to him what the situation was and how he had come to grant the giant the tribute, and told him all the circumstances and the stipulation that had been made between the giant and himself.

Then Tristram said, "If I free you from this thralldom, so that you will never again have to pay this tribute to the giant, what will you give me as a reward?"

The duke replied, "Whatever you like and wish to choose. There is nothing so dear to me that I would not give it to you as a reward if you liberate us from this oppression."

"If you grant me this request," said Tristram, "I shall free you and your country and rid you of the giant and the people of the tribute and free the realm so that it will never again be under coercion."

The duke replied, "I gladly grant your request, and I will confirm this promise before my entire court, which is now here present."

Tristram made ready at once. After putting on his armor and mounting his horse, he said to the duke, "Have one of your men accompany me to the road which the giant will travel, and I shall rid you and your country of the giant. And if I do not succeed in taking vengeance on him on your behalf, I shall not demand the award."

"May God bless you," said the duke, and he ordered one of his men to accompany Tristram as far as the bridge which the giant would have to cross in order to drive the livestock away. Having arrived at the bridge, Tristram proceeded to hinder the cattle from crossing it.

When the giant noticed the fact that his herd had come to a stop, he brandished his iron cudgel and ran as fast as he could until he caught sight of Tristram, sitting in full armor on his horse, and he roared at him in a terrible voice.

"Who are you, churl," he said, "and why do you prevent my cattle from crossing? I swear to you by my head that you will pay dearly for this unless you beg me for mercy."

Then Tristram grew angry and replied, "Never shall I conceal my name from the likes of you, damned troll that you are. At court I am known as Tristram. I fear neither you nor your iron club. You took that livestock unjustly, and for that reason you cannot keep it longer on any condition. Where did you get that great wealth if not by cowing people into paying you tribute?"

The giant Urgan replied. "Tristram," he said, "you are behaving very arrogantly toward me by keeping me from moving my livestock. Get away immediately from me and from the road on which I am accustomed to drive my cattle. I am not Mórold, whom you slew because of your violence, nor am I the Irishman, whom you deprived of Ísönd, and now you intend to treat me the same way. But you can know for certain that you will pay dearly for it if you hinder me in crossing the bridge."

And with that he brandished his iron cudgel and cast it in great anger with all his strength. But Tristram escaped the blow, and the iron staff struck the horse on the chest and smashed it and broke the horse's legs so that it collapsed under the rider.

As soon as Tristram regained his feet, the giant rushed at him quickly to deliver a blow wherever he could get near him and reach him with his hands. When the giant bent down to retrieve his iron cudgel, Tristram did not want to delay any longer, but sprang at him and struck off the giant's right hand just as he was about to pick up the club—and there in the grass lay the hand. When the giant saw his hand lying on the ground, he grasped for his cudgel with his left hand, intending to avenge himself on Tristram. And when he struck at him, Tristram parried the blow with his shield, and the shield split asunder lengthwise into two parts. The blow was so heavy that it forced Tristram to his knees, and he knew that if he received another blow like that, it would kill him, and so he drew back. Since he saw that the giant was seriously wounded and furious and bleeding badly, he decided to wait until the loss of blood wearied and weakened him somewhat. The giant then picked up his hand, and leaving the cattle standing there, made his way homeward to his castle. But Tristram remained behind, hale and hearty and very happy, for now all the livestock had been rescued and turned back.

Tristram now knew for certain that he would receive what he had requested unless the duke broke his promise to him. But it occurred to him that he could not yet return, for he had nothing to show the duke that would prove that he had fought the giant except that he was driving back the cattle. As quickly as he could, he hastened back along the way marked by the blood from the giant's wound. He soon arrived at the giant's castle, and when he entered it, he saw nothing there but the hand. Snatching it up, he hastened back to the bridge as fast as possible. Meanwhile the giant returned to the castle—for he had gone in search of a healing ointment— and assumed that he would find his hand there. After he had laid down the herbs, he discovered that his hand had been taken away. Then he went running after Tristram. Looking behind him, Tristram saw him approaching. He came chasing after him with a great roar and carried his iron cudgel poised on his shoulder. Tristram feared the giant so much that he did not dare advance to meet him. The giant was the first to attack, hurling his iron cudgel at him in great anger and with all his strength. Tristram sprang back so that the blow missed him. Then he rushed at him, intending to strike him on the left side. When he saw the giant twist aside to avoid the blow, he struck him such a heavy blow from the front that it sliced off his arm at the shoulder and hurled him from the bridge so that every bone in his body was broken.

Thereupon Tristram returned, picked up the hand and took it to the duke. But the duke had been in the forest and had watched the encounter between them. When he caught sight of Tristram, he rode out to meet him and asked how things had gone. Tristram showed him his latest accomplishment and told him that he had rescued the cattle and slain the giant. Then he said to the duke, "And now I claim my reward."

The duke replied, "That is right. I shall not deny it to you. Tell me what you would best like to have."

"I thank you very much. I slew Urgan," he said, "and now I wish that you would give me your beautiful dog, which I desire very much to own, for I have never seen a lovelier dog."

Then the duke said, "By my faith, it is true that you have slain our worst enemy, and therefore I will give you half of my realm and an honorable marriage with my sister, if you wish to sue for her hand. But if my dog is more to your liking, you may gladly have it."

Tristram replied, "May God reward you, my lord. There is no treasure in this world as dear to me as the dog, and I shall never give it up for anything else that can be offered to me."

The duke said, "Go now and receive it and do with it as you wish."

CHAPTER 63

More about the dog and Tristram's return.

Once he had received the dog, Tristram did not let it go, nor would he have done so for all the money in the world. He called a fiddler to him, the most courteous man who could be found in the entire duchy, and instructed him in secret what he should do and where he should go and how he should take the dog to Queen Ísönd in Tintajol.

The fiddler journeyed to Tintajol, where he found Bringvet, the queen's attendant. He gave her the dog and asked her to take it to the queen as a gift from Tristram. And she received it from him with great joy and many thanks, for there could never be a more beautiful creature. A house was made for it with great skill from pure gold, and securely locked. This gift was more precious to Ísönd than anything else, and she gave Tristram's messenger a splendid gift as a reward. She sent Tristram word that the king was well-disposed toward him and that he could return without fear since all the suspicions which people had harbored against him had been reconciled and resolved. When Tristram learned this news, he very joyfully returned to King Markis's court.

It was in this way that the dog was procured and obtained. I want you to know, however, that Tristram's dog did not remain long at the court of King Markis. Later he grew accustomed to being out in the woods to hunt wild swine and roe deer when Tristram and Ísönd both lived there. This dog could catch every kind of animal so that nothing ever escaped it, and it was so clever at tracking that it discovered all paths and trails.

CHAPTER 64

Tristram and Ísönd are banished from court.

Tristram had returned to the court of King Markis with joy and gladness, but he had not been there long before the king again discovered the
great love which Tristram and the queen had for each other, now as before.
He was so greatly grieved and distressed at this that he was unwilling to
endure it any longer, and he had them both banished. Tristram and Ísönd,
however, felt that this was an excellent opportunity, and they went out
into the wide wilderness. They gave little thought to who would give them
food and drink, for they felt certain that God would provide them with
nourishment wherever they were. And they were pleased that they should
be together all by themselves. Of all that the world had to offer they
desired no more than what they now had, for they now had that which
pleased their hearts if they might thus always be together without blame
and enjoy their love in bliss.

And as they were pleased with this freedom in the forest, so they found
a secluded place by a certain river in that cliff that heathen men had had
hewn out and adorned in ancient times with great skill and beautiful art.
It was vaulted above, and it had been sunk deep into the earth. The
entrance was underground, and a concealed path deep down led to it.
There was much earth on top of the structure, and on it stood the most
beautiful tree in the forest, and the shade of the tree spread and provided
protection from the heat and burning of the sun. Beside the structure was
a spring with wholesome water, and around the spring grew the sweetest
herbs with lovely flowers that one could wish for, and a brook flowed east-
ward from the spring. When the sun shone upon the herbs, they gave forth
the sweetest fragrance, and then it seemed as though the sweetness of the
herbs mingled like honey with the water. Whenever it rained or was cold,
Tristram and Ísönd remained in the dwelling beneath the cliff. But when
the weather was pleasant, they went to the spring to enjoy themselves and
to those places in the forest that were best for strolling because they were
level and beautiful, or else they hunted game for food, for Tristram had
his favorite dog with him. First of all he trained the dog to catch roe deer,
and then he hunted as many of them as he wished. This afforded them joy
and entertainment, for they had their pleasure and solace night and day.

CHAPTER 65

Kanúest discovers Tristram and Ísönd.

It happened one day that the king, as was his custom, came into the forest with a great company of huntsmen. They unleashed the tracking hounds, prepared blinds, blew their hunting horns to incite the dogs, and ran into the forest in all directions until they found a large herd of deer, from which they separated all the largest animals. Then the deer began to dash in all directions, some up toward the mountains and some down into the valleys, wherever they knew it would be most difficult to track them, and thus the deer left the dogs far behind. But the huntsmen, sounding their horns, went galloping after them.

Then the king left his attendants to follow two of his best tracking hounds, and he was accompanied by several huntsmen who had charge of his dogs. They roused a large stag and put it to flight and chased it eagerly. But it fled as swiftly as it could, in this and that direction, and headed down toward the river. When it came to the banks of the river, it stopped to listen, and heard the pursuit of the hounds behind it, though still far away, and it knew that the hunters were heading straight for it for the attack. Then it doubled back along another path, so that the dogs would not be aware of it, made a great leap over a brook and from there out into the river and then out of the stream again. Because of this the dogs lost the trail and did not know what had become of the stag. And this turn of events vexed the king greatly.

Kanúest was the name of the king's master huntsman. He rode back and forth in order to get the dogs back on the trail, and the dogs hunted far and wide without finding it. Kanúest stopped at the cliff and looked up. Presently he caught sight of the path by the spring, where Tristram and Ísönd had walked early that morning to enjoy themselves. When Kanúest saw the path, it occurred to him that the stag might have passed that way or stopped there to rest. Thereupon he dismounted to ascertain what the situation was. He walked along the path which led to the cliff until he came to the door. He peered inside and espied Tristram and Ísönd sleeping on opposite sides of the room. They had lain down to rest because the heat was so oppressive, and they slept so far apart because they had gone outside to amuse themselves. When he saw them, Kanúest was so frightened that he trembled all over—for there was a large sword lying between them—and he fled to the king and addressed him.

"Sire," he said, "I could not find the deer."

Then he described to the king everything he had seen in the cliff dwelling. He declared that he did not know whether what he had seen was a heavenly or earthly creature or of the race of elves.

CHAPTER 66

The king again receives Tristram and Ísönd into his good graces.

Now the king went there and he saw Tristram and recognized Ísönd and the sword that he himself had once owned. No sword in the world had a sharper edge than the one which lay between the two lovers. Seeing that the two were lying far apart, he reflected that, if there were any sinful love between them, they would certainly not have lain down so far from each other, but would be sharing one bed. Ísönd seemed most sightly to the king, and as he gazed at her countenance, she appeared so lovely to him that he felt he had never seen the like, for she had fallen asleep from weariness, and for that reason her cheeks were flushed. Through an opening in the wall a ray of sun shone on her cheek, and since he was greatly concerned that the sun should shine on her face, he very quietly went to her and laid one of his gloves on her cheek to protect it from the sun. Then he left, and commending them to God, he sadly descended the cliff. The huntsmen ordered the attendants to call the dogs together at once, for the king wished to return home from the hunt. Then he rode alone, grieved and concerned, and no one accompanied him to his tent.

When Ísönd awoke and found the king's glove, she marveled and wondered under what circumstances the glove had come to be there. And Tristram, too, thought it strange. They did not know what they should do now that the king knew where they were. But for both of them it was a great comfort and joy that he had found them in such a manner that he saw them do nothing for which he could reproach them.

And now King Markis was by no means willing to believe that Tristram and Ísönd were guilty of any sin or dishonor. He sent for all of his vassals and showed them cause and reason why the charges and accusations against Tristram were false and foolish, and declared that it would not do for anyone to favor or believe them or to regard them as true. And when they had heard the king's evidence and reasoning, it seemed to them that he wished to bring Ísönd back to court, and they counseled him as they felt and thought best and as his own will was most inclined. And so the king sent for Tristram and Ísönd, and they returned in peace and joy, for he had turned his wrath from them.

CHAPTER 67

The parting of Tristram and Ísönd.

Tristram could by no means restrain his will and desire and therefore he made use of every opportunity he could find. It happened one day that he and Ísönd were sitting together in an orchard, and Tristram held the queen in his arms. And when they thought they were in no danger, an unforeseen event befell them, for the king came into the orchard with the evil dwarf, and he believed that he had caught them in sin, and both were asleep.

As soon as the king caught sight of them, he said to the dwarf, "Wait for me here while I go to the castle to fetch my most distinguished men so that they can see under what circumstances we have found the two of them here. I shall have them burned at the stake if my men see them together."

While the king was saying this, Tristram awoke, but he pretended not to be awake. Then he got up quickly and said, "My dearest Ísönd, wake up, something terrible has happened. We have been tricked and betrayed. King Markis was here and saw what we did, and has gone to his hall for witnesses. If they are able to see us together, he will have us burned to ashes. But now, my most lovely sweetheart, I intend to depart. You need not fear for your life, for no true charges can be brought against you if no one else is found here but you. But I shall go abroad to some other country. For your sake I will endure grief and anguish all the rest of my days. I feel such deep sorrow because of our parting that I shall never find consolation in this life. My sweetest darling, I beg you never to forget me even though I am far away. Love me as much when I am far away from you as you did when I was close to you. You know that I cannot remain here any longer, for those who hate us will soon be here. Now kiss me farewell, and may God guard and protect us."

Ísönd remained there somewhat longer. When she heard Tristram's words and saw his distress, she wept and sighed from the bottom of her heart and replied with sorrowful words.

"My dearest darling," she said, "it behooves you in truth to remember this day on which we part in such unhappiness. I feel such terrible torment at our parting that I have never fully understood before what grief and concern, and care and distress really are. I shall never again find comfort and consolation, nor peace and joy. Never before did I suffer such apprehension for my life as I do now at our parting. All the same, you are to have this finger ring, and guard it well for my sake. It shall be the deed and seal, the promise and the solace of the remembrance of our love and our parting."

And they parted now in deep grief and with a tender kiss.

CHAPTER 68

Tristram travels from country to country.

Now Tristram went on his way. Ísönd remained behind weeping and weighed down with great grief, and Tristram went away weeping much, and leaped out over the orchard fence. Presently the king arrived with his vassals and made accusations against her, but they found no one there except the queen alone. For this reason they could bring no charges against her, and since she had done nothing amiss, the king gave up his anger against her.

Sorrowful, Tristram returned to his quarters and he and all his followers quickly made ready to depart. They rode down to the harbor, boarded a ship, and sailed away from that country. After some time they made land in Normandy, but they did not remain there long. Tristram now journeyed from one country to another to seek for adventures that he might accomplish. He endured many hardships and great fatigue before he attained honor and esteem, and peace and pleasure. Sometime later he served the chieftain and emperor of Rome and remained in his realm for a long while. Thereafter he journeyed to Spain and from there to Brittany to the heirs of Róaldur, his foster father. They received him with great joy, honoring and esteeming him, and consigned without constraint a great realm and many castles to his authority. Loving him with true affection, they helped him in all needs, made him acquainted with strangers, and accompanied him to tournaments, praising his tilting and his valor.

CHAPTER 69

Tristram and Ísodd pledge their troth.

In those days this country was ruled by an old duke, whose neighbors made many attacks and fierce assaults against him. Those who were strongest and most powerful pressed him hard, for they had designs on the castle in which he resided.

This duke had three sons, valiant men. The name of the eldest was Kardín. He was a handsome and chivalrous man, and Tristram's finest companion. Because of his prowess, they gave Tristram a strong castle, from which he was to disperse their enemies. He succeeded so well that he captured many of the enemy, stripped them of their strongholds, and sacked their cities. With the support of Kardín he pressed hostilities against them until they had no other recourse than to throw themselves on his mercy and to sue for quarter.

Kardín had a beautiful, gentle, refined sister who was more intelligent than all other women in this realm. Tristram became acquainted with her and gave her gifts of affection. Because of that Ísönd for whom he grieved, he spoke to her of love and she to him. He composed many beautiful love poems with poetic skill and eloquent wording, and all kinds of lays, and in the songs he often mentioned the name Ísönd.

Tristram sang his songs before his knights and vassals in halls and sleeping chambers, where Ísodd and her kinsmen and many others heard him. All thought that the songs had been composed for this Ísodd, and that he loved no one but her.[1] All of Ísodd's friends rejoiced at this, her brother Kardín most of all, since he believed that Tristram loved his sister Ísodd and that he would remain there because of his love for her. For they had found him to be such a splendid knight that they wished to love and serve him. They had it very much at heart to strengthen Tristram's friendship for their sister, and so they took him to the maiden's apartment so that he might converse with her and enjoy her company, for conversation and entertainment can lead to endearment and can often cause a change of mood. Tristram now devoted much thought to his plans for the future, but he could come to no other decision than that he wished to try to find some pleasure to counter the love which he had so long endured with grief and anxiety and sorrow and distress. For he desired to discover if new love and delight might enable him to forget Ísönd, since he feared that she might have forsaken him, or he wished to take a wife for his pleasure and well-being. So that Ísodd might not reproach him, he wished to marry her for the sake of her name, fame, and deportment. Therefore he wooed Ísodd, the duke's daughter, and with the counsel and consent of her kinsmen was betrothed to her and won her hand. And at this all the inhabitants of the country were delighted.

1. This passage suggests that the names Ísönd and Ísodd were originally and indiscriminately applied both to Tristram's wife and to his sweetheart, and probably also to the queen of Ireland.

CHAPTER 70

The nuptial night.

Now the time was set for the wedding, and Tristram arrived with his friends. The duke was already there with his entourage, and was in agreement with all their plans. The duke's chaplain sang the mass and consecrated the marriage of Tristram and Princess Ísodd in accordance with established custom. Thus Tristram took Ísodd to wife. When divine services were over, they sat down to a splendid banquet. When they had finished eating, they went out to amuse themselves; some took part in jousting, others in the bohort; some cast the javelin, while still others fenced or participated in all kinds of games and pastimes as is the custom of retainers in other countries on such festive occasions.

But as the day drew to a close and night approached, the maiden was conducted to a splendid bed. Presently Tristram came and took off the precious cloak which he had been wearing. When his tunic, which suited him well, was removed, his golden ring was pulled off by the sleeve—the same ring that Ísönd had given him when they had last parted in the orchard, when she had implored him not to violate his love for her. As Tristram gazed at the ring, he once again sank into contemplation, so that he did not know what to do. When he carefully considered his situation, he regretted his decision, and what he had done was now so repugnant to him that he would gladly have made it undone. As he pondered over what he should do, he said to himself: "Tonight I must sleep here as with my wedded wife. I cannot forsake her now, for I married her in the presence of many witnesses. Yet I cannot live with her as man and wife without breaking my word of honor and disgracing myself as a human being. Nevertheless, what is destined must come to pass."

Now Tristram got into bed, and Ísodd received him with a kiss. He leaned toward her and sighed from the bottom of his heart, for he wished to sleep with her, yet could not bring himself to do so—his reason fettered his desire for Ísodd—and he said, "My beautiful beloved, do not find fault with me. I want to tell you a secret, and I beg you that no one know about it except you and me, for I shall tell no one else. I have an ailment on the lower right side of my body that has tormented me for a long time, and tonight this affliction has again oppressed me. Because of the many hardships and sleepless nights I have endured, this old ailment is now disturbing all my limbs so that I scarcely dare lie with you. Each time I suffer a seizure, it brings such a faintness upon me that I am unwell for a long time afterward. Now I beg you—do not blame me for the time being, for we shall have time enough for it when I feel more cheerful and eager."

The maiden replied, "Your affliction causes me more grief than anything else in the world. As for what you want me to keep secret, I can well refrain from speaking about it and shall gladly do so."

Tristram had no other sickness except for the other Ísönd, the queen.

CHAPTER 71

"It is better to have no companionship at all than to have such from which evil comes."

One time when Ísönd, King Markis's wife, was sitting in her sleeping chamber, she grieved and sighed so much for the sake of Tristram, whom she loved above all other men, that she pondered about how she might alleviate her grief and lessen her desire, and found that this was possible only through loving Tristram. But she had had no word of him—in what country he might be, or whether he was dead or alive.

Now there was a huge and haughty giant who had come from Africa to challenge kings and champions. He journeyed throughout many countries in search of them, and he slew and dishonored many and cut off the beards together with the skin from all the chieftains he had slain and made a fur cloak from them, so large and long than it dragged along the ground behind him. This giant had learned that King Artus was so famous in his kingdom that during his day he did not have his equal in courage and chivalry, for he had fought often and against many chieftains and had won victory and renown.

When the giant heard of the bravery and valor of courtly King Artus, he sent an emissary to the king with the message that he had made a skin cloak so long that it dragged on the ground behind him from the beards of kings and dukes, earls and vassals, and that he had traveled throughout many lands to find them and had defeated and killed them in duels and battles. Now since Artus surpassed all he had heard about in both lands and honors, he was sending him instructions in friendship to have his beard cut off and to send it to him as a token of esteem. On his part, the giant would honor his beard so highly that he would place it highest above all the royal beards and fashion from it a border and skin cords, since King Artus was the most famous person he had ever heard about, and for this reason he would esteem his beard most highly.

When King Artus learned this, he grew furious, and he had the giant informed that he would fight rather than surrender his beard like a coward.

When the giant heard the news that the king was determined to fight against him, he hastened at once in a great rage into the border regions of King Artus's realm to fight against him, and the king also proceeded there. Then the giant showed him the cloak he had made from the royal beards. Thereupon they set upon each other with heavy blows and fierce assaults all day from morning until evening, and finally the king overcame the giant and took from him his head and his fur cloak. Thus did the king conquer him with weapons and with valor, and delivered from him the realms of kings and the lands of earls and wreaked vengeance on the giant for his arrogance and malice.

Now, although this does not belong to the subject matter of the story, it is fitting that you know it, for the giant that Tristram slew was the nephew of the giant who had demanded the beard of the king of Spain, whom Tristram was serving. The king of Spain was deeply grieved when the giant demanded his beard, and he disclosed this to his friends and kinsmen and all his knights, but he found no one who had the courage to fight against the giant to protect his beard.

But when Tristram heard that no one dared defend the honor of the king, he undertook the duel to honor the king. Now a very hard battle began with fierce attacks from both sides and Tristram received so many grave wounds that all his friends feared that he would lose life and limb. Nevertheless, he slew the giant. Queen Ísönd heard no news of him, or that he was wounded, for his enviers intervened. It is the custom of those who envy others that they pass over the good deeds in silence, but noise abroad things that are evil. They conceal the fame and courage and achievements of those who are more accomplished than they are, and bring false accusations against the innocent, and conceal their own vices under the slander they utter concerning others. Therefore a wise man instructed his son, saying, "It is better to live without a companion than to be in the company of those who desire evil and always feel hatred, for they conceal the very good that they are aware of. Therefore it is better to have no companionship at all than to have such from which evil comes."

Where Tristram now was, he had enough companions who served and esteemed him, but those comrades of his at King Markis's court were his enemies rather than his friends. They slandered and defamed him and concealed the good things they learned about him because of the queen, who, they knew, was in love with him.

CHAPTER 72

Ísönd learns of Tristram's marriage.

One day, as Queen Ísönd was sitting in her room composing a sad love song, Maríadokk came to her. He was a wealthy man, an earl who owned large castles and prosperous towns in England. He had come to the court of King Markis to serve the queen and to seek the queen's love, but Ísönd told him that with such talk he revealed his folly and that he was pursuing a foolish fancy. He had often implored and hoped for the queen's love, but he had never gained or obtained from her a concession great enough to be worth a glove, for she did not entice him either with promises or with fond words. Yet he remained at the royal court for a long time in the hope that he might mollify her mood for the indulgence of his love. He was a handsome, courtly knight, but otherwise a harsh and haughty man. He was not esteemed for his valor and knighthood, but rather, he was ill-famed as a ladies' man. He, for his part, mocked and made sport of other knights and compared them unfavorably with himself.

One time when he came into the presence of the queen he addressed her, saying, "Lady, when people hear an owl singing, they should give thought to dying, for the song of the owl signifies death. And since it seems to me that this is a sad and sorrowful song, several persons must have lost their lives."

"Yes," said Ísönd, "what you say is true. I wish indeed that this song might signify death. That owl is in truth an evil one that seeks to sadden someone with his own sorrow. You do well to fear your death since you fear my singing. The owl always flies before bad weather, and you always bring bad tidings. You are in truth a flying owl that always desires to tell evil tales and assail one with mockery and ridicule. I know for certain that you would not have come here if you wished to bring me pleasant news."

Maríadokk replied, "Now you are angry, queen. I do not know how foolish one need be to fear your words. I may be an owl, but you must be its bondmaid. However it may be in regard to my death, I do bear sad tidings. You have now lost Tristram, your sweetheart. He has taken a wife in a foreign country, and now you must look around to find another lover, for he has betrayed you and rejected your love. He has married a woman more beautiful and of great distinction, the daughter of the duke of Brittany."

Ísönd replied, "With your ridicule and derision you have always been an owl and a wolf and spoken ill of Tristram. May God never let me thrive if I indulge your desire and folly. Even though you tell me evil things about Tristram, I shall never love you or be your friend as long as I live. I would rather destroy myself than submit to your love."

She grew terribly angry at these tidings.

When Maríadokk realized this, he did not wish to cause her further distress, and so he departed, deeply disturbed that the queen should want to give him such a disrespectful reply.

Now since the queen suffered such grief, distress, and anger, she sought to learn the truth about Tristram, and when she had ascertained the truth, she was overcome with sorrow, grief, and distress and her heart was filled with care and woe. In deep lamentation she said, "No woman can trust a man. Never is it seemly to believe in the love of another. Now he has become a new deceiver by marrying a woman in a foreign land."

Then she bewailed her grief because of their separation.

CHAPTER 73

Concerning the agreement between the duke and the giant Moldagog.

Tristram's situation was a grievous one. And yet he tried to appear cheerful and happy, and never to let people notice that something caused him hurt and harm. He concealed his grief by seeking distraction on hunting expeditions with the duke and his most powerful friends. The duke's son Kardín and two other handsome sons also participated as well as his most powerful vassals. These were to follow the dogs and the huntsmen, but the duke and his sons and Tristram rode along another forest trail down to the sea and looked about to see what might be happening in the borderland, for that is where the boundary was—and they had often fought many battles and fierce skirmishes there in defense of their lands.

In this borderland lived a certain giant who was remarkably huge and most courageous, and his name was Moldagog. He was wise and wily and mighty. And when they had come into this borderland, the duke spoke.

"Tristram," he said, "my dearest friend, here is the boundary of our realm, and our lands do not extend farther into this forest. On the other side of the river a giant owns the forest, and he dwells there in a certain cliff. I want to inform you that this giant was formerly so hostile toward me that he once banished me from my own lands. Since then, however, we have made peace with each other on the condition and stipulation that he shall not come over into my realm and I am not to cross the river into his territory unless absolutely necessary. I want to honor this agreement as long as I can, for if I break the treaty, he has the power to burn and pillage in our lands and to wreak whatever other havoc he can. And if he finds my men on his territory, he has the power to kill them. All my most esteemed men have sworn to observe this stipulation. And if our animals or dogs trespass on his lands, we must effect their return by ransom and not fetch them back and keep them ourselves. I forbid you, Tristram, to cross over this river, for if you do you will immediately be disgraced, destroyed, and killed."

Tristram replied, "God knows, sir, that I have no desire to go over there. I do not know what I should undertake there. As far as I am concerned, he can possess his land without restraint as long as I live. I want no wrangling with him. I shall not be lacking in forest lands during my lifetime."

Nevertheless he gazed into the distance at the forest and saw that it consisted of the finest timber—tall, straight and stout trees of all the kinds he had ever seen or heard named. On one side the forest extended to the sea, and on the other side no one could gain access to it except across the river which flowed there with torrential force—the river which the duke and the giant had formally agreed that no one should cross.

Then the duke turned back and took Tristram's hand, and the two rode side by side, for the duke was very fond of him. Presently they arrived back at the castle, washed their hands, and sat down to table. Later the huntsmen returned with much game.

CHAPTER 74

The campaigns of Tristram and Kardín.

Kardín and Tristram were the best of comrades. They carried on great hostilities and waged war on their enemies who occupied their lands, and they captured large towns and strong castles from them, for they were such valiant knights that nowhere did they find their equals. Powerful princes, vassals, and knights were subjected by them, and they had great power in their realm. They conquered Namtersborg and garrisoned all strongholds in the vicinity of that district with their knights. Consequently the most powerful men sought truces with them, swore oaths, and surrendered hostages to them as surety for a reliable peace.

During all this time, however, Tristram was in great grief and distress because of his love for Ísönd. And he deliberated with all his sagacity on a certain project which he believed he had sufficient time to carry out, for his heart and mind were completely devoted to his love for Ísönd and to all deeds that would redound to her honor.

CHAPTER 75

Tristram invades the giant's forest.

One day Tristram put on his armor and declared that he wanted to go to the forest to hunt, but he later sent his companions and huntsmen away. He had his horse concealed in a certain valley. Taking his horn, he mounted a palfrey and rode very quickly to the place where his war horse and weapons were. And when he had armored himself as best he could, he mounted his charger and rode very swiftly and alone until he came to the ford in the river which separated the realm of the duke from the giant's lands. He saw at once that the ford was very deep and dangerous, and that the river flowed with perilous force and had high banks on both sides. He decided on a difficult course. Whether or not he would ever get out alive, he gave his horse the spurs and galloped it out into the river. The water at once closed over the heads of horse and rider, and he hit the bottom so abruptly that he never expected to get out alive. But he put forth every possible effort, and finally emerged on the other side of the river. He dismounted from his horse and rested for a while; then he took off the saddle and shook the water from it as well as from himself.

And when he was well rested, Tristram mounted his horse and rode into the forest. Setting his horn to his lips, he blew as long and loudly as he could so that the giant would be sure to hear. The giant thought this remarkable, and he wondered what it might be. As soon as he heard the horn he hastened forth, and in his hand he carried a cudgel of the hardest ebony.

When he espied Tristram, in armor and on horseback, he cried out in great anger. "Sir churl," he said, "whoever are you, to sit thus in armor and on horseback? Where have you come from, and where do you intend to go? What do you seek in my hunting forest?"

Tristram replied, "My name is Tristram, and I am the son-in-law of the duke of Brittany. When I saw this beautiful forest, I decided that it is secluded enough to be suitable for a building that I intend to have erected. I see here many varieties of the finest wood, and I shall have the tallest trees, forty-eight in number, felled during the next half month."

CHAPTER 76

The encounter between Tristram and the giant.

When the giant heard and understood these words, he grew angry and replied, "So help me God," he said, "if it were not for the sake of my friendship with the duke, I would kill you with this cudgel, for you are mad with arrogance. Leave the forest at once and be thankful that I let you leave in this way."

Then Tristram said, "Alas for anyone who is pleased with your mercy. I shall have as many trees felled here as I please, and whichever one of us overcomes the other, let him prevail."

Then the giant answered in great anger, "You are a mad, obstinate churl, and puffed up with arrogance. And now you will not escape so easily. You will give me your head as ransom. You think that I am the giant Urgan, whom you slew. No, that is not so. He was my father's brother, and the giant whom you slew in Spain was also a kinsman of mine. And now you have come to Brittany to strip me of my forest. But first you must fight me. If you cannot endure much, your shield will not protect you when I reach you." And with that he raised his cudgel and hurled it at him with great power and fury.

But Tristram evaded the blow and rushed forward to strike him. The giant hastened to recover his cudgel, and there was a sharp exchange of words between them. Then Tristram leaped forward between the giant and the cudgel and tried to strike him on the head, and as the giant reeled backward before the blow, the sword flashed downward into his leg with such force that the leg flew off and landed far from him. And Tristram at once prepared to strike him another blow, on the head.

But at that moment the giant cried out in a loud voice. "Sir," he cried, "have mercy and spare my life. I will become your true and faithful servant and give you all my bags of money. All my lands and all the gold I possess will be placed in your power and at your disposal. I am concerned about saving nothing of mine except only my life. Take me with you wherever you wish and do with me what you will."

As soon as Tristram realized that the giant was begging him for mercy, he accepted his offer of submission, his sworn promise, and his firm pledges. Then he made him a wooden leg and fastened it under his knee, and then the giant was to follow him.

CHAPTER 77

Tristram makes an agreement with the giant.

The giant showed Tristram his hoard of treasure, but Tristram paid little attention to it, for his mind at that time was not much concerned with the acquisition of wealth. Therefore he told the giant that he wished to have no more of his wealth than he needed. Since the giant was bound to him by oath, Tristram let him have charge of his money and keep it in his castle, and they made a new agreement stipulating that the giant should carry out whatever requests Tristram should make of him. And they also agreed that Tristram should have complete disposal of the forest and should have as much timber cut as he wished. Tristram exacted a promise from the giant to tell no one about this. The giant accompanied Tristram to the river and told him where to ride across and took leave of him.

Tristram thereupon continued on his way and acted as though he knew nothing of what had happened. He rode across the ford at the mountain, and got across in such a way that Kardín did not see him. Then he rode back to the court as quickly as he could and said that he had got lost and strayed about in the forest all day, and that he had pursued a large wild boar without being able to catch it. He further said that his bones ached because he had gotten no rest that day, and declared that he was in great need of rest.

When he had finished eating, Tristram went to bed with his wife and lay awake pondering many things. And this surprised Ísodd, and she wondered what could be troubling him and why he sighed from the bottom of his heart, and she asked him what kind of affliction was distressing him so that he could not sleep. She asked him for a long time with sweet and seemly words to tell her about it.

Tristram replied, "This affliction has distressed me since this morning, when I rode out into the forest and roused a wild boar. I inflicted two wounds upon it with my sword, but it escaped nonetheless. This vexed me very much, and I am still angry and annoyed. I rode after it, but it would not stop for me, and in the evening, after I had done all I could, it disappeared into the forest. Now I beseech you, my dearest sweetheart, not to tell anyone about this so that I won't be reproached or rebuked before my companions or the courtiers. This is a great vexation to me, and I intend to ride into the woods at daybreak and search the entire forest. I know by my honor that I shall never give up until I have caught it."

"God knows, my dearest," she replied, "that I shall keep this secret. But beware of others."

CHAPTER 78

The vaulted edifice in the cliff.

At dawn Tristram arose and in secret rode away alone. He succeeded in crossing the river and shortly thereafter reached the giant's castle. The giant strictly honored their agreement, and procured for Tristram craftsmen and all necessary tools, and he did this in accordance with his previous promise. At the place where the forest was densest, there was a round rock completely vaulted inside, hewn and carved with the greatest skill. A stone arch was located under the center of the vault, decorated with carved foliage, birds, and beasts. And under both ends of the arch were such exotic figures that no one who lived there could create anything like them. The vault itself was so constructed all around that no one could enter or leave the edifice except when the tide was at ebb. Then one could walk in or out with dry feet.

A certain giant had come from Africa to construct that vault, and he had lived there for a long time and harried the people of Brittany. He laid waste nearly all the inhabited regions as far as Mt. Michael, which is situated on the seashore. But when King Artus led his army from England to Rome against Emperor Írón, who had unjustly demanded tribute from England, and when King Artus landed in Normandy, he learned what the giant had done and that he had inflicted sundry injuries on people and had devastated almost the entire countryside, so that the king had never before heard of such shameful things. He had also forcibly seized the daughter of Duke Orsl and taken her away with him. Her name was Elena, and he kept her with him in his cave. Because she was a very beautiful woman, he desired to have carnal relations with her. But he was unable to accomplish his purpose because of his huge size and weight, and she suffocated and burst beneath him.

Thereupon Duke Orsl came to King Artus and disclosed his loss and troubles to him. The king was most benevolent and shared the duke's grief at his loss and calamity. When evening approached, the king secretly put on his armor and with two knights set out to look for the giant, and finally found him. But the king alone fought with the giant, and the king had to withstand a fierce onslaught with heavy blows before he succeeded in overcoming the giant. But as far as the story of the giant whom the king slew is concerned, the only part that pertains to this saga is the fact that it was he who built the beautiful vaulted building which pleased Tristram as well as he himself could have wished it.

CHAPTER 79

Tristram engages craftsmen.

Tristram now took advantage of his favorable position in order to have the vaulted edifice renovated and decorated with great skill and all kinds of carved figures, and he kept this secret so cleverly that no one knew where he spent his time or how he occupied himself. He always arrived there early and returned home late, and it cost him much physical and mental exertion to carry out what he had undertaken. He had the entire interior of the building veneered as tightly as possible with deals of the finest wood, and he had all the carved figures colored and gilded with great artistry. And outside, before the door, he had a splendid hall constructed of choice wood, of which there was no lack in the forest. Around the hall he had a secure paling fence erected. In this hall his goldsmiths worked, and the hall was decorated with gold all around so that it was as bright inside as it was outside.

There were artisans of all kinds there, but none of them knew all of

Tristram's plans or why he had had the building constructed on which so many kinds of craftsmen bestowed such great pains. Tristram was so secretive about his project that none of these men knew what he intended or desired to do except what he revealed to the giant, who gave him the necessary gold and silver.

CHAPTER 80

The statues in the vaulted edifice.

Tristram, who found it pleasant beneath the cliff, urged the craftsmen to advance their work as rapidly as possible. Among them were carpenters and goldsmiths, and now everything was compassed and ready to be assembled. Then Tristram permitted the artisans to return home, and he accompanied them until they left the island, whereupon each one returned to his native land.

Now Tristram had no other companion with him except the giant, and the two of them carried the creations of the craftsmen there and assembled the vaulted edifice in accordance with the way the materials had been prepared by the artisans, all colored and gilded with the finest artistry. And there one could plainly see perfect craftsmanship, so that no one could wish for better.

Under the middle of the arch they erected an image so artistic in regard to face and form that no one who looked at it could think otherwise than that there was life in all its limbs, and it was so fair and finely fashioned that in the whole world one could not find a fairer figure. From its mouth there issued such a fine fragrance that it filled the entire building as if all the most precious herbs were in it. This fine fragrance was made to issue forth from the figure by means of a contrivance that Tristram had devised: under the nipple near the heart he bored a hole into the breast and placed therein a small herb container filled with the sweetest gold-mingled herbs to be found in the whole world. Two tubelets of pure gold led from the herb container. One of these tubelets gave forth fragrance from the hairline of the neck, and the other one in a similar manner led to the mouth.

In regard to shape, beauty, and size this figure was so much like Queen Ísönd as though she herself were standing there, and as lifelike as though it were actually alive. This figure was skillfully shaped and as elegantly attired as beseemed the most exalted queen. On her head she wore a crown of pure gold, made with the most skillful workmanship and set with the most costly jewels of every color. And in the foliage, which was attached to the front of the crown on the forehead, there was a large emerald, the like of which was never worn by king or queen. In the right hand of the statue stood a brass wand or scepter, the upper end of which was adorned with the most artistically made flowers. The handle of the scepter was overlaid with gold and set with ring stones. The leaf ornamentations were of the best Arabic gold. On the upper ornamentation of the wand there was a carved bird replete with feathers of many colors and with wings that fluttered as though it were alive and lively.

This statue was clad in the finest purple with fur trimmings. The reason it was clad in purple is that purple signifies the sorrow and sadness, and the misery and trouble that Ísönd had endured for the sake of her love for Tristram. In her right hand she held her ring, on which were engraved the words that Queen Ísönd spoke at their parting: "Tristram, receive this ring in remembrance of our love, and never forget the sorrow, misery and trouble that you have endured for my sake and I for yours." Under her feet was a small coffer cast of copper in the likeness of the evil dwarf who had slandered and defamed them before the king. The statue stood on his chest just as though Ísönd had kicked him under her feet and stepped on him, and he lay supine under her feet just as though he were crying.

Beside the statue was a little toy of pure gold, her dog, which shook its head and rang its bell and was very cleverly made.

On the other side of the dwarf stood a small statue in the likeness of Bringvet, the queen's attendant. The figure was well and beautifully fashioned and clad in the most lovely attire. In her hand she held a vessel with a lid on it, which she offered to Queen Ísönd with a gentle smile. Around the vessel were the words that she spoke: "Queen Ísönd, take this drink which was prepared in Ireland for King Markis."

On the opposite side of the room, near the entrance, he had made a huge image in the likeness of the giant, as though he were standing there one-legged holding his iron cudgel with both hands poised over his shoulder in order to protect the other statues. He was clad in a large, shaggy goatskin. His tunic did not reach down very far so that he was naked from the navel downwards. He gnashed his teeth and had a fierce expression in his eyes as though he intended to crush everyone who entered.

On the other side of the entrance stood a large lion, cast of copper and constructed so cunningly that no one who saw it would have thought otherwise than that it was alive. It stood on its four feet and lashed its tail around a statue made in the likeness of the steward who had slandered and defamed Tristram before King Markis.

No one can report or relate the artistry displayed by these images which Tristram had had made in the vaulted edifice. And now he had carried out for the time being what he had intended, and he entrusted it all to the care of the giant. He had him as his slave and servant to guard everything so well that nothing should come near. But he himself carried the keys both to the vaulted edifice and to the statues. The giant, however, retained all of his other possessions as his own. And Tristram was pleased that he had accomplished all this.

CHAPTER 81

Tristram speaks with his statues.

When Tristram had completed his work, he rode home to his castle, as was his custom, and ate and drank and slept beside his wife, Ísodd, and was pleasant to his companions. But he had no desire to have conjugal relations with his wife. He kept his secret, however, so that no one should discover his design or his deportment, for all believed that he lived with her in a marital relationship as was his duty. And Ísodd was also of such a disposition that she faithfully kept this so secret from everyone that she revealed nothing either to her friends or to her kinsmen. But when Tristram was absent completing his statues, she thought it strange and she wondered where he was and what he did.

Thus he rode to and from his home on a secret path and reached his vaulted edifice without being discovered by anyone. And whenever he came in to Ísönd's statue, he kissed it and took it in his arms and embraced it as if it were alive and spoke many tender words to it concerning their love and grief. He did likewise with the figure of Bringvet, and recalled all the words he had been accustomed to addressing to her. He also remembered all the solace, happiness, joy and gladness he had received from Ísönd, and he kissed her likeness each time he thought of her consolation. But whenever he remembered their grief and the misery and the hardships he had endured on account of those who had defamed them, he berated the image of the evil steward.

CHAPTER 82

Ísodd tells Kardín her secret.

Now when Tristram had come home to his castle, it so happened in this country that Sir Tristram with his companions and Kardín were to travel to a certain holy place to say their prayers, and Tristram had his wife, Ísodd, accompany him.

Kardín rode beside Ísodd on the right side and held on to her horse's bridle, and they chatted about all kinds of pleasant and amusing matters. And as they then rode along with loose reins, the horses went where they pleased and thus they drifted apart. Presently Ísodd seized the reins and gave her horse the spurs. As she lifted her foot from the side of the horse, her thighs were spread apart. Just then the horse skidded into a brook and the water squirted up between her thighs. At this she let out a shriek and laughed at the top of her voice, but said nothing. She laughed so long that she rode for almost half a quarter-mile while laughing, and scarcely gave heed to anything else.

When Kardín saw her laughing in this manner, he thought that she might be laughing at him and that she had heard something foolish or wicked about him. For Kardín was an excellent knight, gracious and chivalrous, popular and courtly, and for this reason he feared that his sister might be laughing at some folly of his. He took offense at her laughter and began to question her.

"What was it," he asked, "that you were just laughing about so heartily? I don't know whether you found yourself or me so amusing. But if you don't tell me the truth about it, you may be certain that I shall have no faith in you henceforth. You may lie to me if you wish, but if I do not ascertain the truth, I shall not love you as my sister."

Ísodd understood what he meant, and she knew that if she concealed the truth from him, she would bring upon herself his hatred and enmity, and therefore she spoke thus.

"Brother," she said, "I was laughing at my own foolish thoughts and at a strange thing that happened to me. My horse leaped wildly into the water, and I was off guard and so some water splashed up between my legs much higher than a man's hand has ever come. Tristram never desires to put his hand there. And now I have told you what made me laugh."

Kardín replied immediately with hasty words. "Ísodd," he said, "what did you say? Don't you and Tristram sleep together in one bed like a pair joined in holy matrimony? Does he behave and live like a monk, and you like a nun? He treats you in an ill-mannered way if his hand never touches you when you lie in bed naked except when he makes love to you."

Ísodd said, "He has never made love to me except to kiss me, and that he does seldom except when we go to bed. I have never known more about the love of a man than a virgin who has led the purest life."

The duke said, "I think that he desires other pleasures than your virginity—that he longs for someone else. Had I known that, he would never have entered your bed."

Then Ísodd replied, "No one must reproach him for this. I expect," she said, "that he will be able to give other reasons. And since he lives in this way, I do not want you to rebuke him for it."

CHAPTER 83

Kardín reproaches Tristram.

When the duke learned that his sister was still a maiden, he was deeply grieved and he deliberated about it, and it seemed to him that this was a dishonor both for him and for all his kinsmen that Tristram did not wish to have an heir from their lineage. He rode on in his sorrow and did not speak about it for the time being because of the persons who accompanied them. And presently they arrived at the holy place where they wished to say their prayers. After they had done this, as seemed fitting to them, they returned to their horses and enjoyed themselves well as they rode homeward.

Kardín harbored angry feelings toward his comrade Tristram, and yet he did not want to discuss the matter with him. Tristram was perplexed and wondered who could have caused Kardín to display such sorrow to him whereas he had formerly discussed everything with him before and afterward. Now Tristram's heart was deeply distressed, and he deliberated how he might ascertain what grounds for complaint he might have.

One day Tristram addressed Kardín. "Comrade," he said, "what is the meaning of this? Have I done anything to offend you? I can sense that you harbor great anger toward me. Tell me clearly and truly what the cause is so that whatever is wrong can be righted. It seems to me that you speak disapprovingly of me both in my presence and in my absence. There is neither merit nor nobility in hating and scorning me against my deserts."

Although angry, Kardín replied courteously. "I will tell you this," he replied, "that if I do hate you, it befits no one to reproach me or my friends and kinsmen either if they should all become your enemies unless you are willing to make amends. For the shameful offense you have committed against me by disdaining the maidenhood of my sister—and this concerns all who are her kindred and friends—is a dishonor to us both at court and elsewhere. For my sister is such a gentle maiden that it beseems no man, however courtly and highborn, to disdain her. Therefore it would be no reproach or disgrace to you to love her as your wedded wife and to live with her in a matrimonial relationship. But we all know now that you do not wish to have a legal heir from our family. And if the comradeship between us were not so firm and steadfast, you would pay dearly for this dishonor which you have inflicted upon my dearest kinswoman. In my entire realm she has no equal in beauty and gentility and all those accomplishments which it beseems a woman to possess. Why were you so bold as to dare to marry her, when you did not wish to consummate the marriage and live with her as a husband should with his wife?"

CHAPTER 84

Tristram pleads his defense.

When Tristram had listened to Kardín reproaching him, he replied with harsh and angry words. "I have done nothing that it was unseemly for me to do. You speak much about your sister's beauty and gentility and noble lineage and her many accomplishments. But now you may know for certain," he said, "that I have a sweetheart so beautiful and noble, so genteel and wealthy and praiseworthy that she has in her service a maiden so beautiful and gentle, so wealthy and highborn and so skilled in every kind of accomplishment, that it would be more fitting for her to be the queen of the most splendid king than for your sister Ísodd to be the lady of a castle. And from this you can understand how splendid and exalted this lady must be, to have such an attendant. I do not say this to disparage you or your sister, for I admit that your sister is beautiful and gentle, of good lineage and wealthy in possessions. But she cannot compare with my dearest, who surpasses all other living women. To her I have dedicated all my desire with such devotion that I am powerless to love Ísodd."

Then Kardín replied, "Your tricks and lies will avail you nothing unless you show me the maiden you praise so highly. And if she is not as beautiful as you say, you shall make amends to me, God willing, and I will bring about your death. But if the maiden you praise so highly is as you say, you shall remain unmolested by myself and all my kinsmen."

Tristram understood Kardín's threats and his anger and he pondered over them, but he did not know what he should do, for he loved Kardín more than any other of his friends and therefore did not want to cause him any more grief under any circumstances. Yet he feared that if he told him his secret he would reveal it to his sister. But if he did not tell it to him, he would be destroyed and deprived of life, deceived and disgraced, whether rightly or wrongly, for Kardín could certainly bring about his death by craft or cunning.

Presently he said, "Kardín, my dearest friend. You have made me acquainted with this country, and through your furtherance I have received manifold honors. If I have offended you, may I suffer harm at your hands if that is your intention. But I shall neither desire nor cause grief and distress to arise between us through any deed I may commit, considering that this is very much against my inclination. Now since you wish to know my plan, love, and secret, which no one except me knows about, and if you wish to meet the beautiful maiden and see her famous appearance and apparel and converse with her, it is my request, for the sake of our fellowship, that you do not betray this secret and private matter to your sister or to anyone else, for under no circumstances do I want her or anyone else to learn about it."

Kardín replied, "You have my promise and my word of honor that I shall never betray anything you wish to be kept secret, nor reveal anything without your consent. Now tell me about it."

Now each swore faithfulness and fidelity to the other and made it binding that Kardín should keep everything secret that Tristram was willing to tell him.

CHAPTER 85

Tristram takes Kardín to the vaulted edifice.

One morning very early Tristram and Kardín secretly prepared to leave the city, and all those who remained behind wondered where they intended to go. And at daybreak they set out and followed their course through forest and wilderness until they came to the ford in the river, and Tristram made as if he wanted to ride across. And when he had entered the ford, Kardín cried out in a loud voice.

"Tristram," he called, "what do you intend to do?"

Tristram replied, "I want to ride across the river and show you what I have promised you."

Then Kardín grew angry and said, "You want to deceive me and deliver me into the power of the giant, our worst enemy, who kills everyone who goes there. You are doing this instead of keeping the agreement you made with me. If we cross the river, we shall never return alive."

When Tristram perceived that Kardín was afraid, he blew his horn four times, as loudly as he could. In this way he signaled the giant to come there. And presently the giant appeared on the other side of the river on the cliff, as angry as though he were in a fury and swinging his cudgel. He cried out to Tristram in a dreadful voice. "Tristram," he said, "what do you want of me that you summon me so vehemently?"

Tristram replied, "I wish to ask you to permit this knight to accompany me wherever I want to go, and to throw away your iron staff." The giant did so at once.

Then Kardín began to take heart and rode across the river to Tristram. Tristram told him about their dealings, how they had fought and he had cut off the giant's leg. Then they rode on until they reached the top of the mountain, where they dismounted and then walked up to the building. Tristram unlocked the door, and at once they were engulfed in the sweet fragrance of balsam and of all the sweetest herbs there. When Kardín caught sight of the likeness of the giant standing near the door, he was so frightened that he almost lost his wits, for he believed that Tristram had betrayed him and that the giant would kill him with his poised cudgel. And because of this fear and the fragrance that filled the room, he was affected so strangely that he fell into a swoon.

Tristram raised him up and spoke to him. "Let us," he said, "go to where the maiden is who serves the splendid lady with whom, as I told you, I am very much in love."

But Kardín was completely in fear and terror and seemed to be frantic in his mind and deprived of his reason. He glanced at Bringvet's statue and thought it was alive. But he was in such great dread of the giant—and his eyes dwelt mostly on him—and because of this he could not see otherwise than that the statue was alive. Meanwhile Tristram went to the likeness of Ísönd, embraced and kissed it, and spoke to it in a low tone of voice and whispered in its ear and sighed like one who is deeply in love.

Presently Tristram spoke to the statue. "My most beautiful sweetheart," he said, "because of my love for you I am sick both night and day, for my whole desire and all my longing completely comply with your wish and will."

Sometimes he was very sad and in an angry mood when he spoke, but sometimes he seemed to be in good spirits.

CHAPTER 86

Tristram and Kardín sail to England.

Kardín was deeply impressed by this and he said, "Tristram, it would be fitting for me to receive some benefits too, seeing that there are such beautiful ladies here. I admit," he said, "that you have a most beautiful sweetheart. Make me a partaker of your joys by letting me be the lover of the queen's attendant. For if you do not keep the promise you made me when we rode away from home, you will suffer reproach because of it."

Thereupon Tristram took him by the hand and led him to Bringvet's statue. He said, "Isn't this maiden lovelier than your sister Ísodd? If it so happens that there is talk about it, be sure to bear witness to what you got to see here."

Kardín replied, "I see that these are exceedingly beautiful, and therefore it is fitting for you to share their beauty with me. We have been comrades for such a long time that it is proper for us to be partakers of both of them."

"Yes," exclaimed Tristram, "I choose the queen. But you take her attendant. I give her to you."

Kardín replied, "May God reward you for treating me so kindly. That is proof of friendship and comradeship."

Kardín looked at the golden vessel in her hand. He thought it was filled with wine, and he wished to receive it from her. But the vessel was so cleverly and skillfully secured and glued to her hand that he could in no way take it. When he looked more closely, he discovered that both were images, and he turned to Tristram.

"You are a clever man," he said, "and full of wiles, to deceive and trick me, your steadfast friend and devoted companion. But if you do not show me the women in whose likeness these statues were made, you will have dealt falsely with me and completely broken our agreement. But if you show me those creatures who resemble these images in appearance and beauty, you will have deported yourself honorably, and then I shall be able to believe what you say. And now I want you to give me the maiden as you gave me her likeness."

Tristram replied, "That shall surely be if you will keep your word to me."

They renewed their mutual pledge on their word of honor and with confident courage. Then Tristram showed Kardín everything there, colored and carved and gilded and grooved in with such versatile handicraft that never before had the human eye seen the like. Kardín was amazed, and wondered how Tristram could have accomplished all this. Presently Tristram locked the building and they returned home.

After they had rested at home for several days, they both made ready to visit a holy place. They set out with their pilgrim staffs and satchels and took no one with them except two kinsmen, handsome men, courageous and keen with weapons and accomplished in all courtly customs. They took complete outfits of armor along, and told the court retainers and all the people that they took their weapons along because they feared criminals and evil men in a strange land. In a short while they took leave of their friends, set out on their journey, and made for England. Each of them longed for his beloved, Tristram to see Ísönd and Kardín to see Bringvet.

CHAPTER 87

Tristram and Kardín meet their sweethearts.

Now when Tristram and Kardín had come so far on their journey that they would soon reach the city in which King Markis was to spend the night, and since Tristram was thoroughly acquainted with the countryside there, they rode toward the king's entourage, although not on the same road but rather along secret paths. And presently they espied the royal retinue riding in their direction, a great number of men.

When the king had ridden past, they caught sight of the queen's attendants. Thereupon they dismounted near the road and left the horses in the care of the pages. Both of them walked toward the carriage in which Ísönd and her attendant Bringvet were sitting and they came so close to the wagon that they could greet the queen and her attendant politely. Ísönd recognized Tristram immediately, and at once she grew sad, thinking about the great love she had enjoyed for a long time. But Bringvet gazed greatly enamored at Kardín. But because the queen's carriage was accompanied by a large body of knights, the queen feared that Tristram could be recognized by the king's men if they tarried there. So she quickly took the gold ring that had always been carried back and forth between them by messengers and tossed it to Tristram with these words: "Ride away from here, strange knight, and find quarters for yourself, and do not delay our journey."

And when Tristram saw the ring, he recognized it and understood the queen's words, and both he and Kardín returned to their pages. They rode away from the king's and queen's entourage, but yet they had knowledge of their journey until the king arrived at the castle in which he took lodging for the night. When the king and queen had finished dining and drinking in courtly fashion, the queen was the first to leave. She went to the room where she was to sleep that night privately with her attendant Bringvet and the maid who served them. But the king slept that night in another building with his confidants.

Now when the king and his whole company had gone to bed, Tristram and Kardín were hiding in a secluded wood near the castle. They told their pages to remain there and guard their horses and armor until they returned. They went to the castle in disguise to determine where the queen's room was, and then entered secretly and knocked on the door. Queen Ísönd sent her maidservant to see whether some poor man might have come there to beg for alms. And when the servant opened the door, Tristram bowed to her, greeting her with pleasant words, and he immediately took the gold ring that Ísönd had given him and bade her take it to her. Ísönd recognized it at once and sighed. Tristram conducted Kardín into the room. Tristram quickly took Ísönd into his arms and kissed her with great tenderness and joy. Kardín went to Bringvet and embraced and kissed her lovingly. When they had spent a long time in this manner, drinks and all sorts of dainties were brought for them. Then they went to bed. In this very night Kardín took his sweetheart into his arms with ardent love. But she took a silk pillow, made with marvelous skill and craft, and placed it beneath his head; and immediately he fell asleep and did not wake up during that night. Thus the two, Kardín and Bringvet, slept together that night.

Kardín did not awake until morning. He looked around and at first did not know where he was. When Kardín discovered that Bringvet had already arisen, he realized that he had been tricked because he had awoken so late. Ísönd took to teasing and jesting with him, but Kardín became very angry because of Bringvet although he did not reveal it very much. They all spent the day together very agreeably.

In the evening they went to bed. Bringvet again put Kardín to sleep in the same manner as before, and when day came, he awoke in the same way.

The third night Ísönd did not wish for Kardín's sake that he should be deceived any longer, and their intercourse was very joyful. So long did they all remain there together with great delight that those who envied them discovered their doings. Yet they were warned early enough so that they could take precautions. Tristram and Kardín went away secretly, but it was not possible for them to return for their weapons and horses.

CHAPTER 88

Maríadokk routs Tristram's pages and mocks Bringvet.

Maríadokk the steward was the first one to discover the horses. And when Tristram's pages, who were guarding the horses, realized what was happening, they rode away at once, taking the shields and armor with them, and they heard behind them the shouts and cries of their pursuers. Maríadokk, who was closest to them, saw the pages fleeing and thought that it was Tristram and Kardín. He cried out in a loud voice and said, "Under no circumstances shall you escape, for on this day you shall lose your lives and then leave your bodies as hostages. Shame to such knights," he continued, "to flee from us like this. It is not fitting for the king's knights to flee, either because of fright or for fear of death. Haven't you just come from your sweethearts? Indeed, you disgrace them most shamefully." Such were the words spoken by the steward.

The pages galloped the horses as fast as they could go.

When Maríadokk and his companions no longer wished to chase them, they returned to quarrel with the queen and with Bringvet, her attendant. And after they had belabored them for a long time with shameful words, Maríadokk began to mock Bringvet. "Last night," he said, "you shared your bed with the most craven and cowardly knight who has ever come into this world. It is very fitting for you to have such a lover, who flees from knights as a hare before the hounds. I shouted to him in a loud voice many times and with many words, asking him to wait for me and to defend himself against me, but he didn't even dare to look back. Shamefully do you squander your love when you bestow your favors on such a knave. Why did you grant your affection to such a fainthearted knight? But you have always been so misled and confused that I have never been able to show you any kindness or good will."

CHAPTER 89

Bringvet relates her grief.

When Bringvet had heard so many scornful words, she spoke out in great anger. "Whether he is courageous or cowardly," she declared, "I prefer him for a lover to your false beauty. God grant that he never gain power over anyone if he is even more cowardly than you, and he certainly displayed cowardice if he ran away from you. You have no right to blame him, for many find more to condemn in you. But whatever you say about him regarding his running away, it may yet come to pass, God willing, that you will learn whether or not he will flee before you. God knows that I cannot believe that he would run away from you or that you would dare look at him in an angry mood and with ill will. For Kardín is such a valiant and powerful man and such an excellent knight that he would no more flee from you than a greyhound from a hare or a lion from a he-goat."

Maríadokk replied, "Both fled like cowards. But where does this Kardín come from? He had a shield newly gilded all over and decorated with leafy design and his horse was dapple grey. And if I see him again, I shall recognize both his spear and his standard."

Bringvet realized that Maríadokk had recognized Kardín's shield and banner, his horse and armor, and she was vexed because of this. She left him angrily and presently found her lady, Queen Ísönd, who was sorrowful for the sake of Tristram. She spoke to the queen in grief and anger.

"Lady," she said, "I am dying from grief and sorrow. I must rue the unhappy day on which I came to know you and Tristram, your sweetheart. For your sake and his I deserted both kinsmen and friends, and I gave up my native land and my virginity because of your folly. God knows that I did it for the sake of your honor, and not for my own pleasure. But as for Tristram, that evil perjurer—may God bring him such disgrace this very day that he may lose his life—, for it was his fault that I suffered disgrace in the beginning. Don't you remember that you wished to have me killed in the forest like a thief? It was not your doing that your thralls spared me. Their hatred was better for me than your friendship. How foolish I was to be willing to trust you again or to cherish any feelings of love for you from that time on."

Bringvet sharply reproached the queen volubly and with serious accusations and enumerated for her all their dealings and rebuked her for all the offenses committed against her by both of them.

CHAPTER 90

Tristram returns from the forest.

When Ísönd heard how distressed and angry Bringvet was, and when she renounced her friendship—to whom she had formerly been so dear and devoted in this life, and who guarded her honor beyond all other living persons—her joy turned to sorrow and sadness and all her pleasure was destroyed. Bringvet spoke very abusively and put her to shame and provoked and depressed her greatly so that Ísönd was so vehemently afflicted with a twofold affliction that she could not free herself from it regardless of what she did. She sighed deeply and spoke from the anguish of her despair.

"I am miserable," she said, "and more wretched than all other creatures. Why should I have lived so long to endure such deep woe in a strange land?"

And Ísönd now reproached Tristram severely with harsh words and blamed him for all her misfortune and all the grief and distress she had endured until then, and also because Bringvet had become so terribly angry and had denied her her friendship. And yet Bringvet was not willing to disgrace her before the king because of Tristram, and matters remained thus for some time.

As Tristram and Kardín were in the forest together, Tristram considered how he might learn to his complete satisfaction how matters stood with Queen Ísönd and Bringvet. He swore an oath that he would not return until he had ascertained if anything had happened to Ísönd. He bade his companion Kardín good day and returned by the same path on which they had ridden from the castle. He picked a certain herb and ate it, and his face swelled up as though he were ill. Both hands and feet turned black and his voice became as hoarse as though he were a leper, and for this reason he could not be recognized. He took a goblet that Ísönd had given him during the first winter he had loved her, and then he went to the royal court and stood by the gate and listened to the talk about events at court and begged for alms.

CHAPTER 91

Tristram is driven away.

Since a certain festival had arrived, the king was on his way to the cathedral and Ísönd walked next to him. When Tristram saw that, he at once hastened after them, shaking the goblet briskly and begging for alms, and he followed her as closely as he could. Distinguished men, who accompanied the queen, were greatly amazed at him and pushed and threatened him because he was walking so close to her and was so persistent in his entreaties. But if he had wished to use his strength, he could have quickly avenged himself; and so they shoved him out of their company and threatened to beat him. But he begged all the more and refused to turn back despite their blows and threats. He called persistently to the queen, but she was filled with grief and sorrow. Presently she looked back at him with angry eyes, and she wondered what kind of man he might be. And when she recognized the goblet and saw Tristram, her mood suddenly changed, and she took off her finger ring. She did not know how to give it to him, and she tossed the ring into his goblet. But Bringvet was nearby and recognized him by his stature, and she spoke to him as though in anger.

"You are a dolt," she said, "and a foolish rascal and so ill-mannered that you force yourself upon the king's vassals and have no respect for his courtiers." Then she said to Ísönd, "What has just come over you that you so abundantly give such great gifts to such people? You refuse to reward distinguished people, and yet you give this man a gold ring. Take

my advice. Don't give him anything, for he is an imposter and a fraud."
Thereupon she told Tristram's enemies to drive him away from the
church. They shoved him unmercifully, and yet he endured it.

Tristram now knew that Bringvet was angry with him, and likewise
Queen Ísönd, and now he was disgraced even more in many respects. At
the royal court there was a stone hall that lay quite in ruins because of
age and neglect. Under the steps of this hall Tristram sought shelter,
lamenting his grief and feeling oppressed from toil and fatigue. He would
rather die than live, for no one was willing to help him.

Queen Ísönd was deep in thought, and she cursed the entire time during
which it was her lot to love a man so ardently.

CHAPTER 92

Tristram and the castle guard.

When the king and queen had heard mass, they went to the table and
dined, and on this day the king was merry and cheerful. Ísönd was sad
and filled with anxiety.

Somewhat later it so happened that the man who guarded the king's
castle and all the doors to it lay awake until far into the night. The weather
was severe and he felt cold, and so he asked his wife to make a fire so that
he might warm himself. She went out for dry firewood, and came to where
Tristram lay underneath the stone wall, tormented by the cold. As she
searched for wood, she touched his cloak, which was all damp from the
frost. She was frightened and thought that it must be something evil, for
she knew that no one had ever stayed there before. She asked him who he
was and where he had come from, and he told her, entrusting her both with
his name and where he had come from and what his intentions were. Her
husband was very fond of Tristram, for he had done him many favors
while he lived in England. When the castle guard learned that Tristram

was there, he went to him at once and brought him to his home, where he prepared both a fire and a bed for him and everything else that he needed.

CHAPTER 93

Tristram and Kardín wreak vengeance and return home.

Queen Ísönd called Bringvet to her and spoke to her with affectionate words.

"I beseech you," she said, "to forgive Tristram and to go to him and console him somewhat in his distress. For he will die if he receives no help, and I shall always love him."

Bringvet replied, "From now on I shall never again console him in his distress. Rather would I desire his death. Nor am I any longer willing to acquiesce to your sins. He has shamefully dishonored me."

Ísönd said, "It is not seemly for you to gainsay me or to quarrel with me or to reproach me. God knows that I have always regretted what I have done against you, and therefore I beseech you to be of some help to him, lying there as he does."

Ísönd implored Bringvet so long with fair and fond words that at last she was unable to refuse her request. She arose and went to the place to which she had been instructed to go. And when she arrived there, she found Tristram downcast and joyless because of what had happened and for many other reasons. He asked why she was angry with him, and she frankly told him all the reasons. He assured her that his comrade Kardín would soon come there on such a mission as would prove him to be un- deserving of any reproach. She believed his words and felt greatly relieved, and then in mutual trust they proceeded to the queen's room, where they found a warm and affectionate welcome. Tristram spent the night there in good cheer. In the morning he received the queen's leave to depart, and they parted in great sorrow.

When Tristram reached his companion Kardín, he suggested that they go together to the royal court for a while to see whether anything of interest was happening there, and they disguised themselves carefully.

At that time the king was celebrating a festival, and a great multitude had come there, both rich and poor. When the people had finished eating and the tables had been removed, all the courtiers went to view or participate in the entertainment, and there were all sorts of games. First they performed the dance called valeys. Then they hurled the javelin, and took part in other contests in which they were skilled. Tristram far surpassed all the others in valor and accomplishments. Next to him Kardín was praised most highly. A certain companion of Tristram who recognized him in the contests at once gave him two chargers, the best of all the king's stallions (and in all England there were no fleeter horses), which had often been tried in battle. For he feared that if they were recognized, they would be betrayed.

Presently they took part in a bohort. Tristram and Kardín were well versed in the use of weapons, and pressed their opponents hard, thrusting many of them from their horses. They too took great risks, for they killed the two most powerful men in the country. There Maríadokk was slain by Kardín, who thus wreaked vengeance on him for lying about him and saying he had fled before him.

Thereafter they departed and both comrades together rode rather swiftly to the seashore, where their companions were all ready to sail. And because Tristram and Kardín turned off the road there, those who had pursued them now headed for home. Thereupon they turned back and slew many, but did not wish to pursue them. Tristram and Kardín then embarked, hoisted sail, and sailed out onto the sea. They were merry and happy that they had avenged themselves so well.

CHAPTER 94

Tristram the Dwarf appeals to Tristram for help.

Not long thereafter they made land in Brittany, and their friends and members of the court were there to greet them. After they had returned home, they often went on hunts and to tournaments. Everywhere they gained victory and fame above all others in Brittany because of their chivalry, valor, versatility, and nobility. They often went to where the statues were to pass the time there and for the sake of those whom they loved so dearly.

One time as they were riding homeward and had just left the forest they saw a knight riding in great haste on a fawn-colored horse. They wondered where he wanted to go since he was riding so swiftly. He had an excellent suit of armor and was splendidly clad and equipped. His armor was made with fine craftsmanship and completely gilded. He was a tall man, well proportioned, and very handsome. Tristram and Kardín waited for him since they wanted to know who he was. Before long he rode up to them. He greeted them with courteous and cordial words, and they answered him respectfully and chivalrously. They soon asked him who he was, where he came from, and what his mission was since he was riding so swiftly.

The knight said, "I desire greatly to find that man whose name is Tristram."

Tristram said, "What do you want of him, since you ask about him in this way? You have come very close to him. If you want to take lodging with him, come along home with us and share our hospitality."

He replied, "I shall certainly do so. I am a knight and live here in the borderlands of Brittany. I am called Tristram the Dwarf—a misnomer, for I am a huge man, and I had command of a castle and was married to a beautiful, wealthy lady whom I love deeply. But evening before last I lost her, and therefore I am anxious and angry. Now I do not know what to do unless someone comes to my support. And so I have turned to you, because you are so famous and valiant, wise and well loved by your friends, but fierce to your enemies. I need that you proffer me some wise counsel and help me in my extremity and that you try to return my wife to me. In return I shall be true and faithful to you and become your liegeman."

Tristram replied, "I shall gladly help you. But first you must come home with us and spend the night there. And in the morning, I shall indeed accompany you."

CHAPTER 95

Tristram is wounded with a poisoned sword.

At the break of day Tristram and his companions made ready and set out on their way. The strange knight rode at the head of their band, and he did not halt until they reached the castle where the evil and arrogant man lived. He had seven brothers, all of them fierce and malevolent knights.

Not far from the castle Tristram and his companions dismounted from their horses and awaited coming events. At three o'clock in the afternoon two of the brothers rode out of the castle, and as soon as they caught sight of Tristram and his brothers, they vehemently set upon them with eagerness and ill will. A skirmish ensued, and the outcome of it was that Tristram and his companions slew both brothers. One of the other brothers discovered what had happened and at once raised the war cry. And when those in the castle heard it, they armed themselves and rode out and at them. These men defended themselves skillfully and bravely, but it was a hard fight. And Tristram and his companions slew the seven brothers and their company, more than one hundred foot soldiers. In this battle Tristram the Dwarf was slain, and Tristram sustained a wound from a poisoned sword. But Tristram made the man who had wounded him pay dearly, for he slew him.

This wound was so severe that Tristram was able to reach his castle only with great difficulty. And then all the physicians in the country were summoned, but they were unable to bring him any relief, for they did not know how to treat poisoned wounds or to draw out the venom, as was necessary.

CHAPTER 96

Tristram sends Kardín to fetch Ísönd.

Tristram's affliction worsened from day to day, for no one there could help him. The venom spread throughout his entire body and all his limbs, and from this he was greatly harmed. And now he declared that he must soon die unless help came to him quickly.

He considered now that no one would be able to bring about a cure except Queen Ísönd, his sweetheart, if she came to him, for he could not have himself taken to her. He sent word to Kardín, asking him to come to him alone.

Ísodd, Tristram's wife, was very curious to know what designs he might have—whether he wished to become a church dignitary or a monk or a cleric. She also wanted to ascertain what plans they devised. Therefore she stood outside by the wall near which Tristram lay in his bed in order to hear their conversation through the wall, and she posted guards to prevent anyone from seeing her.

Presently Tristram raised himself and rested on the pillow, and Kardín sat beside him. They lamented their grief and spoke much about the mutual love and fellowship they had enjoyed for such a long time and about the great deeds of valor they had accomplished. And now both of them realized that they would soon be parted, and they wept together about the parting.

And Tristram then said, "If I were in my own country I would receive help there from someone. But here in this country no one is sufficiently skilled, and therefore I must die from lack of help. I know no living being who can cure me or be of assistance to me except Queen Ísönd in England. If she knew of my condition, she would provide some expedient, for she possesses the most knowledge and the greatest will. But now I do not know how she is to learn about this. If she knew, she would certainly bring me some relief. No one in the world is so well versed in the art of medicine or in all the courtly crafts that it befits a woman to possess. Now I want to request of you, my dear companion Kardín, for the sake of our love that you go to her and tell her what has befallen me, for there is no one whom I trust as I do you, nor is there anyone whom I love as deeply as I do her, and no one has done so much on my behalf as she. For you promised this to me with a sworn oath when Queen Ísönd gave you Bringvet at my request. Now do as I beseech and expect of you. And if I recover, I shall reward you as richly as is possible and proper."

Now Kardín saw that Tristram was very downcast, and all of this caused him anguish, and he said, "I shall gladly go to her and do everything you want me to if it be God's will that I bring it about."

Tristram thanked him and said that he should take his ship and represent himself as a merchant when he arrived there. "Take my gold ring along as a token," he said, "and show it to Queen Ísönd at the first opportunity. And then she will know where you have come from and will be willing to speak to you privately. And tell her what has happened and what has befallen me, and ask her to prepare a quick and effective expedient if she desires to help me."

Now Kardín made quick and thorough preparations for the voyage with as many men as he wished. Before they took leave, Tristram implored him at great length to make all possible haste and to bear repeatedly God's and his own greetings to Queen Ísönd. Then each embraced the other, and Kardín with a favorable wind put out to sea.

Now Ísodd, Tristram's wife, felt certain that he loved someone else more than he loved her, for she had heard their entire conversation, but she pretended to know nothing about it.

Now Kardín sailed across the sea and made land where he had intended to in England. He and his men now posed as merchants and busied themselves both buying and selling, and had hawks and other wares for sale. Kardín put a goshawk on his wrist and a piece of precious cloth on his arm and went thus to the king's castle. Kardín was an eloquent man, courtly and well-mannered, and he addressed the king courteously and with cordial words, saying, "My companions and I are merchants, and we should like to request your permission to anchor in your harbor and to have safe conduct while we are in your realm."

The king at once granted the request and bade them welcome and promised them safe conduct. Thereupon Kardín presented the king with three gifts.

After that he went to the queen and greeted her courteously and politely and gave her a golden brooch so lovely that it could not have been lovelier. Thereupon he took two rings and showed them to her and asked her to choose one of them. She looked at the rings and immediately recognized Tristram's ring. She trembled all over and her heart sank, and she changed color and sighed heavily, for she felt certain that she would learn such tidings as would be of no consolation to her. Because of the other people who were present she pretended that she wished to buy the ring rather than to accept it as a gift. Presently she and Kardín went aside to speak in private. He gave her Tristram's greeting with fair words and warm feeling and told her that Tristram's life and death were in her power. "He is your faithful lover in every respect." He reported to her in a few words the events that had befallen them and about Tristram's situation and sickness, and that nothing awaited him but death unless she went to him as quickly as she possibly could.

When Ísönd heard this news about the torture and torment of both of them, she was filled with sorrow and confusion. She quickly called Bringvet to her and told her what she had learned about Tristram, that he was confined to his bed with mortal wounds, and that there was no one in that country who knew how to heal him—and she asked for her counsel. Bringvet replied that she should make ready as quickly as possible and leave with Kardín as soon as evening came and take everything she needed with her.

And when night had fallen and all the people at court were asleep, they left the castle by means of a secret door that they knew about; Kardín joined them immediately, and they hastily went down to the harbor and onto the ship, hoisted the sail, and sailed away from England with the most favorable wind they could hope for. They were all merry and cheerful, and looked forward to something quite different from what was in store for them.

CHAPTER 97

Ísönd and Kardín are tossed about on the high seas.

Now we must turn the story back to Tristram. He now suffered greatly both from the pain of the wound and from the grief caused by the fear that Queen Ísönd would not come to him and that no one in that country would be able to assuage his distress. He often had his men stationed along the shore to see whether anything approached land. Sometimes he had himself carried down to the seashore when he could not trust anyone else. Nothing in the world did he desire so much, neither food nor drink nor anything else, than to see and to talk with Queen Ísönd.

And now he got to hear the cruel news. When Ísönd and Kardín had come close to land, a violent tempest arose against them and swept them away from land and back onto the high seas. For many days and nights they were on the high seas, so forcibly held offshore that they scarcely hoped to escape alive.

Then Queen Ísönd gave vent to her grief and said, "Now it is not God's will that I should see Tristram alive or solace him in his distress as I desire to do. Alas, my dear friend and sweetheart! If I now perish at sea, there will not be a living soul in this world who will be able to heal your wound and save you from death. Now I would desire that God willed, as I do, that, if I were to die here, your death would unite us."

Such laments and many others did Ísönd utter. But her crew greatly feared that they would perish in the storm.

CHAPTER 98

The ship is becalmed.

Now Ísönd was deeply concerned, more for Tristram than for herself. For ten days they were tossed about by this violent tempest. Then the storm abated, the weather cleared, and a favorable breeze sprang up. They hoisted sail and the following day approached land as they had done before. But then the breeze died down and the ship drifted to and fro offshore, and they had no boat since it had been smashed. And now their perplexity and distress increased once again because they could not reach land. Ísönd was so dismayed at this that she was nearly undone by it. But those who waited onshore could not see the ship, and longed greatly for those who had sailed away.

CHAPTER 99

The death of Tristram.

Tristram's grief and melancholy had now increased so greatly that, sighing, he was quite exhausted, and sometimes he lost consciousness because of Queen Ísönd, whose arrival he so desired.

Then his wife, Ísodd, who had devised an evil scheme, came and spoke soothingly to him. "Dearest," she said, "Kardín has arrived. I have seen his ship for certain, and it has only a light breeze. May God let it bear good tidings and bring you comfort."

When Tristram heard her words, he raised himself up at once as though he were well and spoke to her. "Dearest," he said, "are you quite certain that it is his ship? If this is true, tell me with what kind of sail he is sailing."

She replied, "I can see quite clearly that they are sailing with a black sail. They have no wind, but are drifting back and forth offshore."

But she had lied to him, for Kardín was sailing with hoisted white and blue gleaming sails, for Tristram had asked him to do so as a sign that Ísönd was with him. But if Ísönd had not come with him, he would have sailed with a black sail. Ísodd, Tristram's wife, had heard all this when she had concealed herself behind the wooden wall.

When Tristram heard this, he was afflicted with grief such as he had never before suffered. He turned toward the wall at once and cried out in a grief-choked voice, "Now you hate me, Ísönd. I grieve because you will not come to me, and I die for your sake since you would not take pity on my affliction. And now I grieve and mourn my affliction because you would not come to comfort me."

Thrice he called his beloved Ísönd, naming her name, and the fourth time he surrendered up his spirit and his life.

CHAPTER 100

Ísönd goes ashore and learns of Tristram's death.

The knights and squires who were present were deeply grieved at Tristram's death, and all the inhabitants of the city mourned him in great sorrow. They lifted his body from the bed and laid a cover of costly cloth over it.

And then for those in the ship the breeze began to grow stronger, and they sailed into the harbor. Now when Ísönd had left the ship, she heard the people sobbing in great sorrow and tolling all the bells. She asked why the people behaved so sorrowfully, and what tidings they had heard.

An old man replied to her. "Lady," he said, "we suffer grief so great that never before has such sorrow befallen us. Tristram, the valiant and courtly, lies dead in his bed. Never before has such sorrow come upon this country."

When Ísönd heard this, she was so deeply moved that she was unable to speak, and she threw off her cloak. The Bretons wondered where this beautiful woman had come from and from what country she might be.

CHAPTER 101

The death of Ísönd.

Queen Ísönd now went to where Tristram's body lay on the floor, and turning to the east offered up her prayer with these words: "I beseech Thee, almighty God, be merciful to this man and to me inasmuch as I believe that Thou wast born into this world of the Virgin Mary for the redemption of all mankind, and inasmuch as Thou didst help Mary

Magdalene and endure death for us sinful people and that Thou didst suffer Thyself to be nailed to the cross and to be pierced with a lance in the right side, and didst go harrying to Hell, whence Thou didst redeem all Thy people into eternal bliss. Thou art our Creator. Eternal, almighty God, look with mercy on our sins inasmuch as I will believe all this. And I will gladly believe and I will gladly praise and worship Thee. And grant, I pray Thee, my Creator, that my sins be forgiven, one God, Father, Son, and Holy Ghost. Amen."

"Tristram," she said, "I love you deeply. And now that I see you dead, it is not fitting for me to live any longer, for I see that you died for my sake. And therefore I shall not live after you."

Then she spoke many words about their love and life together and their sorrowful separation. Thereupon she lay down on the floor and kissed him and laid her arms around his neck. And as she did so, she breathed her last.

Tristram died so quickly because he thought that Queen Ísönd had forgotten him. And Ísönd died so quickly because she came to him too late.

Hereupon they were buried. It is said that Ísodd, Tristram's wife, had Tristram and Ísönd buried on opposite sides of the church so that they would not be close to each other in death. But it came to pass that an oak tree[1] grew up from each of their graves, so high that their branches intertwined above the gablehead of the church. And from this it could be seen how great had been the love between them.

And thus ends this story.

1. The text reads *eik eða lundur*, "an oak tree or a tree." This is evidently an emendation made by an Icelandic scribe.